Spoof

GUY PIRAN

First published in Great Britain in 2006 by
Allison & Busby Limited
13 Charlotte Mews
London W1T 4EJ
www.allisonandbusby.com

10 9 8 7 6 5 4 3 2 1

ISBN 0 7490 8196 1
978-0-7490-8196-6

Printed and bound in Wales by
Creative Print and Design, Ebbw Vale

Acknowledgements

Dedicated to GCP & JRC
and the young pretender,
Luke Jack Sumner-Stanger

Many thanks to...

Lizzy & Lucy Mole, Mark Harden, Joe Stanger and Julia Dunlop
for their love, support and friendship

Foreword

On the 27th July 2004 two thousand letters were posted on a circuitous drive through Sussex. Three days later the police came looking for me.

In retrospect I should never have created the good-natured but completely barmy Anne Wayward, headmistress of the equally fictional Brighthelm Primary School, nor ever engendered the notion of the Dangerous Sports Club. Fortunately, once the police realised that Anne Wayward and her entourage of innocent five-year-olds were entirely fictional, and would not be jettisoned from aeroplanes, marched to the South Pole, cast out upon the ocean waves, or left to languish at Her Majesty's Pleasure, and that there was positively zero chance of Kimodo Dragons being recklessly released on a Hebridean island, they were prepared to see the funny side of a writer trying to make his way in the world.

My thanks to those who entered into the spirit of Spoof, along with all those who unwittingly contributed. We live in an all too serious world at present, where there is, I believe, much need of a little light relief.

May the Spoof be with you.

Guy Piran

Alexander Literary, Film and Television Agency

148 Montpelier Road, Brighton, East Sussex, United Kingdom, BN1 2LQ.

Ken Livingstone,
Greater London Authority,
City Hall,
The Queen's Walk,
London,
SE1 2AA

Dear Ken,

I am writing to you as the managing director of the Alexander Agency. We represent a number of clients in the entertainment industry. One such client is Michael Roedenberg who is a German conceptual artist. His work usually involves large-scale outdoor installations and it is with one such projected installation in mind that I am writing to you in this instance.

Michael would like to have an enormous prophylactic made up (a Bavarian rubber moulding company have already agreed to undertake its creation). With the use of a helicopter he then wishes to deposit the huge condom directly over Nelson's Column in Trafalgar Square. If the manufacturers have been precise regarding their measurements the large rubber ring at the base of the condom should come to rest about a metre from ground level. The whole installation of the piece should only take a few minutes.

We envisage that the work would remain up for a period of a few hours to allow film and photographs to be taken, and also to allow the general public to admire what will be a record-breaking length of latex. After a sufficient length of time Michael with the help of a number of assistants will then mount the rubber ring around the base. With a good deal of combined jumping they then hope to force the nipple at the peak of the condom to split over Nelson's head. Once the latex is torn it will simply be a case of pulling the membrane down to the base of Nelson's Column. The large rubber ring can then be cut and the whole used condom removed by lorry from the square.

Michael would, however, like to know if it would be possible to leave the spent condom around the base of the column overnight and in addition to this to add a reasonably convincing amount of opaque, viscous liquid around the rubber and over a little of the paving stones beside the column. He would be hoping to have this spectacle filmed early the next morning before its final removal.

Perhaps you could get in touch with me to discuss this matter further.

Yours truly,

Guy Piran.

(Managing Director)

GREATER**LONDON**AUTHORITY
Finance & Performance

City Hall
The Queen's Walk
London SE1 2AA
Switchboard: 020 7983 4000
Minicom: 020 7983 4458
Web: www.london.gov.uk

Our ref: MGLA020804-4988
Your ref:
Date: 03 August 2004

Guy Piran
148 Montpelier Road
Brighton
East Sussex
BN1 2LQ

Dear Mr Piran

Thank you for your letter to the Mayor of London regarding Nelson's Column. I have been asked to reply.

The GLA has considered your proposal, but feels that Nelson's Column is not an appropriate location to be used as part of your proposal. The proposal of placing a giant condom on Nelson's Column would conflict with the Heritage values of the Square.

Nelsons Column is a listed monument, where any structure must be carefully considered in the context of protecting the fabric of the square, and surrounded on all sides by busy roads, where drivers may be distracted by the proposed artwork.

Yours sincerely

Paul Cavanagh
Project Officer

148 Montpelier Rd,
Brighton,
East Sussex,
BN1 2LQ.

Dear English Heritage,

I am writing to you as head of the Mosley International Procurement Agency based here in the UK. An American casino corporation has recently approached me with what amounts to an extraordinary request.

In February 2005 the newest and most up-to-date gaming facility will be opening in Las Vegas. It is to be called the Stonehenge Casino and when completed will dwarf many of its competitors, such as the Sahara and the MGM. The whole hotel and casino complex is being built out of stone slabs the size of station wagons. When complete, both inside and out will be left with a rough-hewn stone effect. Although the Griffin Corporation will not comment in any more detail, I believe that even the guests bedrooms will be entirely fitted out with stone - stone beds, rock-hewn shower units, etc. There is even rumour that they are having 1000 slot machines crafted entirely from solid blocks of granite. I am also led to believe that all casino gaming chips are going to have been crafted from different types of rock.

All in all this new casino is going to be one of the most extraordinary of its type in the entire world.

What the Griffin International Corporation would dearly like for their opening night is to have Stonehenge shipped over to them to stand in the enormous hotel lobby. At first I though their wishes preposterous, but they have convinced me otherwise. They are willing to hire the entire archaeological departments of two reputable West Coast universities to help facilitate any movement of the ancient monument. Along with this they would be hiring one of the most prestigious construction companies to oversee the movement of the aforementioned Stonehenge. They would be using the most sophisticated of equipment in order to facilitate this manoeuvre and would have the stones duly flown via the use of enormous Russian transport planes to Las Vegas itself. They would hope to have them there for just one week and then have them flown directly back again.

Whilst they are gone from the traditional site in Wiltshire they would be replaced with what I am led to believe will be extremely convincing facsimiles.

It seems to me like one hell of a length to go, but the Griffin Corporation prides itself on no-expenses barred enterprises. To this end I have no doubt that they would pay a small fortune to English Heritage if you were to accede to their requests.

If you could get back to me on this I would be most grateful.

Yours truly,

Edward Wallis.

ENGLISH HERITAGE

04 August 2004

SOUTH WEST REGION

STONEHENGE

Mr E Wallis
Mosley International Procurement Agency
148 Montpelier Road
BRIGHTON
East Sussex
BN1 2LQ

Dear Mr Wallis

STONEHENGE CASINO

Thank you for your letter (undated) which has been forwarded to me from Customer Services regarding the request for Stonehenge to be transported to Las Vegas for the opening of the Stonehenge Casino in February 2005.

It sounds a very interesting and fascinating project. However, as Stonehenge has been standing at its current location since it was built more than 3,500 years ago, it is not possible to consider moving the stones under any circumstance.

If you wish to discuss your project further, please do not hesitate to contact me.

Yours sincerely

Peter Carson
Head of Stonehenge

148 Montpelier Rd,
Brighton,
East Sussex,
BN1 2LQ.

27.07.04

Portchester Crematorium,
Upper Cornaway Lane,
Portchester,
Hampshire,
PO16 8NE

Dear Sir or Madam,

I am writing to you with what you will no doubt consider to be a somewhat peculiar request. Some Twelve months ago my husband died in a tragic accident. After the funeral service he was duly cremated at the Aberdeen Crematorium. I have since relocated to Brighton where I now live, and I have kept my husbands ashes in a large pot near the fireplace. It is only recently that I have started having problems.

At first I though it must be mice, because I live in an old house and rodents inevitably get under the floorboards. That would account for the persistent scratching sounds. However, it can in no way account for what has now become a persistent, albeit reasonably quiet, knocking. This knocking can go on for hours and always seems to occur at night when I am trying to watch television. Although infrequent, I have also on occasion heard a faint, high -pitched metallic moan, somewhat like the buzz of a fly but much more melancholic.

Would it be possible to have Arthur cremated again? There's not a lot of him now, and I can't imagine that it would take you very long to do. I had thought of just putting him in my domestic oven, but somehow it just doesn't seem very dignified, nor, for that matter, very hygienic. I am happy to pay full cremation rates if need be, but I would hope that because of Arthur's reduced nature you could, in turn, make a reduction yourself.

I look forward to hearing back from you.

Yours truly,

Edna Burton.

Portchester Crematorium Joint Committee

J Clark M.Inst.B.C.A.
Manager & Registrar

ask for

your reference

in reply please quote

Portchester Crematorium

Upper Cornaway Lane
Portchester Hampshire PO16 8NE
Telephone (01329) 822533

29TH July 2004

Mrs E Burton
148 Montpelier Road
Brighton
East Sussex
BN1 2LQ

Dear Mrs Burton

Thank you for your recent letter to which I must say it is one of the most intriguing situations I have ever encountered.

My first thoughts are on the matter are whether re-cremating your husband will actually "cure the problem." There are also technical difficulties in cremating already cremated remains and that is not to lose them in the actual process.

Whilst I am not actually against the idea in principle I think you may consider that having the remains buried in a local church/cemetery or in some significant spot this may be a way of finally laying Mr Burton to rest.

If you would like to discuss this further please feel free to telephone on the above number.

Yours sincerely

J Clark
Manager & Registrar

11

Seeboard PLC,
PO Box 5050,
329 Portland Rd,
Hove,
East Sussex.

148 Montpelier Rd,
Brighton,
East Sussex,
BN1 2LQ.

Dear Sir or Madam,

I am writing to you because I am very concerned and worried. Last Thursday I had the misfortune to drop a porcelain teacup onto the floor near an electric plug socket. While I was on my knees clearing up the broken crockery I became aware that I could hear voices. These voices were coming from the electric plug socket. At first I thought that I had gone completely potty, and I tried to seek out a rational explanation. Could it have been the next-door neighbours behind the adjoining wall? I went next door and rang their bell. There was no one there and the curtains were closed. I returned to the plug socket and the voices were there, strong as ever.

I went to the kitchen to put the kettle on. I was, to say the least, a little shaken. But then moments later I realised I could hear voices coming from the socket in the kitchen. In alarm and a certain amount of panic, I plugged the toaster into the vacant socket where the voices were coming from. For a moment I could not hear any voices but then I distinctly heard muffled cries coming from behind the plug. I didn't know what to do. Suddenly I grabbed both plugs and pulled them out of their respective sockets. Moments later I could distinctly hear a multitude of tiny, high-pitched gasps of relief. I'm sure I even heard a squeaky little voice saying something like 'phew, that was a close one!'

Within a few moments I had my coat on and I was walking by the sea. I stayed out of the flat all afternoon. When I returned the voices were still there, and I felt like I had no choice but to unplug everything in the entire flat, even important items such as the fridge, washing machine and cooker. With each pulled plug I heard similar gasps of relief as I had heard with the toaster and the kettle socket. Half an hour later I had disconnected every plug in my flat, and the noise, although hardly what I'd call deafening, was still quite unbelievable. It was like a hundred thousand tiny people were having a party. There was singing that sounded a little bit like birdsong, and laughter that sounded like millions of mice being squeezed. To my mind these 'little people' behind the plug sockets were celebrating some kind of freedom from captivity. I have not plugged anything back in since then for obvious reasons.

What am I to do? I cannot live with just lighting alone, and the last thing I want to do is cause mass suffering to persons unknown. Do you think I should talk to the sockets and explain my position? I have not wanted to do this yet because I think that way madness lies. I am hoping that you have some prior experience of the predicament I find myself in, and that you can offer me some sound advice. I dearly hope you can get back in touch with me as soon as possible.

Yours sincerely,

Mrs Primrose Sainthouse. (Retired).

SEEBOARD

Customer Service
Gadeon House
Grenadier Road
Exeter Business Park
EX1 3UT

T 0800 3289010
F 01392 813650
E Pete_pearce@edfenergy.com
   Minicom 0800 3289013

Mrs P Sainthouse
148 Montpelier House
Brighton
East Sussex
BN1 2LQ

Our ref	Your ref	Extension	Date
PRP		714 3683	2nd August 2004

Dear Mrs Sainthouse

Thank you for your recent letter regarding the problems you are experiencing with your electricity supply. Mrs Sainthouse, if you would to discuss this matter in more detail I can be contacted on Freephone 0800 3289010.

I look forward to hearing from you.

Yours sincerely

Peter Pearce
Priority Services

Alexander Literary, Film and Television Agency

148 Montpelier Road, Brighton, East Sussex, United Kingdom, BN1 2LQ.

The British Library,
96 Euston Rd,
London,
NW1 2DB

Dear Sir or Madam,

I am writing to you as the managing director of the Alexander Literary, Film and Television Agency. At the moment I have the pleasure of representing the Chilean writer Ernaldo Cortez. Ernaldo is working on a new book, which we hope to have placed with publishers by the summer of 2005. With close reference to writing by the Marquis de Sade, this novel depicts the disintegrating relationship between a poverty-stricken pig farmer and his once 'well-to-do' wife.

As well as drawing upon illustrations in de Sade's work, Ernaldo has benefited from viewing Nineteenth Century pornographic photography. I stress that he has taken no great satisfaction or pleasure in doing this, and that he has done this purely in terms of professional research. Ernaldo has recently been in contact with me at my agency to ask me whether I might be able to track down two extremely rare 19th Century imprints for him to view. Knowing the British Library's record in storing material, I have written to you in the first instance, but perhaps if you do not have these items in stock then I will contact the Bodlean in Oxford.

The first book Ernaldo would like to view is titled 'Sexual Gratification in the Pursuit of Pleasure' and seems to have been written by a certain Arthur Mosely. The book is rumoured to contain over 60 photographic plates featuring Arthur and many of his servants, both male and female. I am told that the last two plates deal entirely with his favourite hounds.

The second book was written by Walter Finch and is called 'Living with Monkeys Has Not Made Me Happy'. I am uncertain as to whether there are photographic prints that accompany this book or just illustrations.

Ernaldo would dearly like to be able to view both these works in their entirety if you have them available. If not, are there any other books that you could recommend that deal explicitly with 19th century pornography and preferably have plenty of illustrations and/or photographs?

I should be most grateful if you could get back to my agency on this matter.

Yours truly,

Guy Piran.

BRITISH COLLECTIONS 1801
EARLY PRINTED COLLECTI

96 EUSTON ROAD
LONDON NW1 2DB
Telephone 0171–412 7604

our ref
your ref
date 2 August 2004

Dear Mr. Pirân,

Your undated letter, received by us on 29 July, on two certain books. The Private Case, an annotated bibliography of the Private Case erotica collection here, does not list either Mosely or Finch. Our catalogues say the same story. I have looked at COPAC, an union catalogue unifying the on-line catalogues of 24 "major" university libraries in the United Kingdom and Ireland. It does not list either Mosely or Finch. Evidently both books are indeed rare and quite out of sight.

I would suggest that these books be looked at:

Patrick J. Kearney: The Private Case: an annotated bibliography of the Private Case erotica collection in the British (Museum) Library, London, 1981. No plates but a good source on pornography. The books listed are available by and large for inspection

Patrick J. Kearney: A history of erotic literature, London, 1982. This has plates, illustrations and — importantly — a bibliography.

Yours sincerely,

R·J. GOULDEN

15

148 Montpelier Rd,
Brighton,
East Sussex,
BN1 2LQ.

Cinder Hill Equine Clinic Ltd,
Cinder Hill Lane,
Horsted Keynes,
Haywards Heath,
West Sussex,
RH17 7BA

27.07.04

Dear Sir or Madam,

I am writing to you in the hope that you may be able to help me. I have a pet goldfish called Slurpy who is on his last legs, as it were. He's been going downhill for some time, and now he seems to have hit rock bottom. All his once golden colour is drained and his eyes wear a continual glazed look, as if he's now somewhere distant and remote. I do not give it very long before Slurpy finally goes to the great blue beyond.

I shall miss Slurpy very much. Even though we have not known each other for a great length of time I still felt that there has been a bond between us that has kind of bridged once-incommunicable areas of the animal kingdom.

At first I thought that Slurpy was just gulping in water to oxygenate himself, and obviously some of the time this was all that he was doing. But at other times I knew he was talking to me. I would have my face right up against the side of the goldfish bowl making polite conversation, and Slurpy would be talking right back to me. These conversations have now sadly ceased.

I heard all about Dolly the sheep while watching a television programme and a thought occurred to me there and then that if you can clone a whole sheep then why not a tiny little goldfish. Do you think that there's any possibility of me being able to have it done with Slurpy? Perhaps you could accomplish this in-house at the surgery? Does Slurpy still have to be alive in order to be successfully cloned, or would a few of his scales be sufficient? I don't really think that he'll last beyond next month, so I hope that his scales will do.

My wife thinks I should stop being so soppy and sentimental, but what does she know? When you've found a friend who you can talk to for hours on end, and who's conversation never gets boring, you don't want to lose that friendship. I will happily pay for Slurpy to be cloned again and again and again just to keep our friendship intact.

I do hope that you will be able to help me in this matter or, perhaps, refer me to the relevant bodies that can. Thank you for your time.

Yours truly,

Stanley Smith.

CINDER HILL EQUINE CLINIC LTD

VETERINARY SURGEONS:
CHRISTOPHER D. GINNETT, B.V.M.& S., M.R.C.V.S.(Principal)

MICHAEL J BARROTT, B.V. Sc., Cert. E.P., M.R.C.V.S.
DEBORAH A. WALKER , BSc.,(Hons) MA., VetMB., M.R.C.V.S

CINDER HILL LANE
HORSTED KEYNES
HAYWARDS HEATH
WEST SUSSEX
RH17 7BA

Telephone: 01342-811335
Fax: 01342-811404
E-mail: cginnett@cinderhillvet.plus.com

Ref: CDG/jd

04th August 2004

Mr S Smith
148 Montpelier Road
Brighton
East Sussex
BN1 2LQ

Dear Mr Smith,

Thank you for your letter of 28th July regarding 'SLURPY'.

By coincidence, my colleague Michael Barrott is particularly interested in cloning and will be pleased to advise and assist you in as far as the current state of the procedure is possible. I understand from him that the recovery of DNA material is best achieved from a living subject but, although a little more complicated, the result can be achieved from sample material.

I have already informed him that you may be contacting him and suggest that you either telephone or write to him at the above address at your convenience. It did occur to me that a simpler option would have been to procure a Mrs SLURPY but I realise that this might dilute the genetic material which you particularly wish to achieve.

With kind regards

Yours sincerely

C D Ginnett BVM&S, MRCVS

17

148 Montpelier Rd,
Brighton,
East Sussex,
BN1 2LQ.

Channel 4 News,
ITN,
200 Grey's Inn Rd,
London,
WC1X 8XZ

Dear Channel Four Television,

I am writing to you to make an official complaint. I have been watching Channel Four Television ever since its inception, and I particularly like the in-depth news programme that comes out in the early evening. However, I must take issue with one of the presenters of the aforementioned programme - one John Snow. I have absolutely no problem with the manner in which he presents the programme, and I find his frank questioning of current politicians and experts in their field to be of a robust and searching nature. This is all that I require in a professional news presenter.

What I do not require, however, is night after night being confronted with brightly coloured, garish ties that give me incessant headaches. Does anybody in the production team realise the harm these ties can have on people with 'delicate' sight? I suspect not, because otherwise Snow would have been told to ditch the carousel for a more fitting and sober variety.

I have actually been to my doctor about this and he told me that I should either adjust my television set so that it performs in black and white only, or contact Channel Four directly. I do not see why I should have to view the news in black and white at the beginning of the Twenty-First Century. Incidentally, I have experimented with this colour-draining procedure and found my headaches simply replaced with a certain irritation at the pattern of the ties. It is only in black and white that the truly hideous nature of these patterns becomes apparent.

Perhaps it wouldn't be half so bad if Snow was to wear the same tie for each broadcast. One, perhaps, could get used to the garishness and the harsh symmetry after a while. But this is obviously never going to be the case because he wears a different and never-before-seen tie every damned time he presents the news.

What can Channel Four do about this intolerable situation? Presumably some of you think Snow is being trendy and avant-garde? That's what television people are like, isn't it? I should like to see Snow wearing single-coloured and calming pastel shades of tie, and even on occasion - god forbid! - a dark coloured tie. Is this really asking so much?

I sincerely look forward to hearing your response.

Yours truly,

Miriam Smithson.

200 Gray's Inn Road
London WC1X 8XZ
Telephone (020) 7833 3000

03.08.04

Dear Miriam Gilbertson,

The man is an incurable recidivist — a fetishist obsessed with neck-wear — his attended endless therapy and treatment sessions at assorted institutions — these have only served to infect his journalism let alone the ties.

Do continue to watch this space

Warmest regards

Jon Snow

Registered Office 200 Gray's Inn Road London WC1X 8XZ Registered Number 548648 England
Independent Television News Limited

Alexander Literary, Film and Television Agency

148 Montpelier Road, Brighton, East Sussex, United Kingdom, BN1 2LQ.

Lost Property Office,
200 Bakerloo Street,
London,
NW1 5RT

Dear Sir or Madam,

I am writing to you with regard to a somewhat urgent matter. I am the managing director of the Alexander Agency here in Brighton. I help to run a busy production company and we are at present helping to set up a new London show of Snow White and The Seven Dwarves. The show itself is being performed and acted by a Ukrainian drama troupe who use monkeys dressed up as dwarves as opposed to 'vertically challenged people'.

Sadly one of their entourage went missing on the Circle Line last Thursday and has not been seen since. Have you by any chance taken in 'Sleepy'? At first glance he would look like the archetypal dwarf, but closer inspection would no doubt reveal a rather incongruous tail. 'Sleepy' is in no way dangerous, and out of all the monkeys he is the least trouble in terms of maintenance.

However, my colleagues and I and, indeed, the remaining members of the Ukrainian drama troupe are now thoroughly concerned about our disappeared monkey. Is there any possibility that he is at this moment still travelling around on the Circle Line? By this time he would undoubtedly by severely distressed and in desperate need of water.

We are presuming, in fact, that he has not been found as this would by now have undoubtedly drawn the interest of the press. Could he perhaps have disembarked from the circle line and unwittingly entered into the tunnels themselves? We would be most grateful if you could contact us as soon as possible in order to clarify the position and if in fact 'Sleepy' has been found and, perhaps, handed over to the RSPCA.

Yours sincerely,

Guy Piran

Transport for London
Lost Property Office

Transport for London
Lost Property Office

200 Baker Street
London NW1 5RZ

Phone 020 7918 2000
Fax 020 7918 1028
www.tfl.gov.uk

Our ref: JH / 7

Mr Guy Piran
Alexander Literary, Film and Television Agency
148 Montpelier Road
Brighton
East Sussex
BN1 2LQ

29 July 2004

Dear Mr Piran

RE Lost Property

Thank you for your recent enquiry regarding the loss of your monkey that goes by the name of Sleepy. We are unable to keep animals at this office therefore should your monkey have been found the British Transport Police would have been informed by the Station Supervisor and then it would be collected by the RSPCA.

May I suggest that you contact the RSPCA to see if Sleepy has been handed in to them?

I am sorry that I am unable to assist you any further.

Yours sincerely

Jennifer Humphreys
Support Manager

A division of Transport Trading
Limited whose registered office is

Windsor House
42-50 Victoria Street
London SW1H 0TL

Registered in England and Wales
Company number 3914810

VAT number 756 2770 08

Transport Trading Limited is a
company controlled by a local
authority within the meaning of
Part V Local Government and
Housing Act 1989. The controlling
authority is Transport for London

The Stuffed Spouse Society

148 Montpelier Road, Brighton, East Sussex, BN1 2LQ.

Bluebell Railway PLC,
Sheffield Park Station,
A275,
East Sussex,
TN22 3QL

Dear Sir or Madam,

I am writing to you as the chairwoman of the Stuffed Spouse Society based here in Brighton. As the title of our society suggests, membership is restricted to those who have had occasion to have their spouses stuffed. At present our membership is entirely female but we hope to find the odd husband or two in the future who have had their spouses stuffed too. We would not want to be seen as a sexist organisation in any way. As it happens, however, having one's spouse stuffed does seem to be a more feminine pastime.

Our calendar for 2005 is positively filled full of good ideas - a day on Blackpool beach, walking in the Chilterns, a visit to Madame Tussauds in London - but we would definitely also like to come down to Sussex and see the sights. While there we would like to make use of your Railway for a day's outing. Would it be possible to rent an entire carriage to ourselves? There would be twenty living spouses and twenty stuffed ones, making a total of 40 in all. If there was a shortfall in numbers expected to be seated in the carriage we would be more than happy to make up the deficit in terms of payment.

As you can imagine stuffed spouses are not everyone's cup of tea, and without a carriage to ourselves we may cause unintended alarm or distress to other paying passengers. This is the last thing that we would wish to happen. In terms of any embarkation and disembarkation all our stuffed spouses are properly mounted on sturdy plinths. They each have two-wheeled trolleys of the variety used in commercial warehouses, which means that they can easily be transported along platforms, etc. When in transit the stuffed spouses are always covered with special body-socks. These socks are usually of a calm and sober grey colour so as not to draw attention to the covered stuffed spouse.

May I also take this opportunity to assure you that all the aforementioned stuffed spouses must come up to the highest standards of taxidermy before membership is offered. There is absolutely no 'home-made' stuffing allowed whatsoever, whatever the skills of the spouse are. All stuffing must be done by professional and long established firms.

What this means is that there are no health concerns whatsoever in the context of our stuffed spouses. They each come with taxidermist's certificates specifying their clean bill of health. It is also our society policy to have these bills of health renewed on a yearly basis, a little bit like a car M.O.T.

We would like to hire a carriage sometime during the week of 5th to the 12th of June, for both an outwards bound and return journey. I would be most grateful if you could tell me whether it would be possible to accommodate our society during this period. Could you also include in any such correspondence the rate of fares for the forthcoming year, 2005.

Than you very much for considering my request.

Yours truly,

Bertha Sykes (retired).

BLUEBELL RAILWAY PLC

SHEFFIELD PARK STATION, A275, EAST SUSSEX, TN22 3QL

Talking Timetable: 01825 722370 General Enquiries: 01825 720800 Fax: 01825 720804
Catering Dept. and Pullman Bookings: 01825 720801 Catering Dept. Fax: 01825 720805
Web site: www.bluebell-railway.co.uk email: info@bluebell-railway.co.uk

4th August 2004

Bertha Sykes
The Stuffed Spouse Society
148 Montpelier Road
Brighton
BN1 2LQ

Dear Bertha

Re: Group visit to The Bluebell Railway 2005

Thank you for your letter regarding a group visit by your society to the Bluebell Railway. I am happy to confirm that subject to the dates that your require we would be able to let you have a whole carriage for your exclusive use providing, of course, that you paid for the maximum number that the carriage holds i.e.64 and we would require payment in advance to secure the booking.

The cost would be £8.00 per person (stuffed or otherwise) depending on the age at which they were stuffed as we do give senior citizen discounts. If you advise me of the actual dates that you are thinking about then I can make the necessary arrangements.

As you say in your letter we would need you to keep your stuffed spouses covered whilst boarding so that small children and those of a delicate disposition are not unduly alarmed and I am afraid that we will not have enough platform staff on duty to help with pushing the trolleys on which your spouses are mounted so you would have to arrange this yourselves. Under 'Railway Regulations' paragraph 3, section 5, sub-section 2a appertaining to the transit of stuffed spouses, appropriate certificates should be provided for inspection on the day of travel, attached securely to the relevant spouse for the duration of the journey.

I hope this letter answers your queries but please free to contact me if I can be of further assistance.

Yours sincerely

Ivor Thaun

Bluebell Railway

The Stuffed Spouse Society

148 Montpelier Road, Brighton, East Sussex, BN1 2LQ.

09.09.04

Graham L. Flight,
Bluebell railway PLC,
Sheffield Park Station,
East Sussex,
TN22 3QL

Dear Sir,

Thank you for responding so speedily to my letter of enquiry. I am delighted that you can allocate a whole carriage for our Stuffed Spouse Society outing, and we will be more than happy to pay for the full allocation of seats.

As I stated before there will be twenty stuffed and twenty living spouses, making a total of forty in all. This leaves a shortfall of 24 which we will be happy to pay at the full adult rate. I am also extremely impressed that you make allowance in terms of senior citizens discounts for those spouses that died above a certain age.

Only two of our stuffed spouses died before the age of sixty-five (Albert Renwick and Edward Smithkins), though both of their respective living spouses are now of senior citizen age. Therefore only Albert and Edward will have to pay full adult rates.

We would like to book your carriage for the 7th June 2005 for both an outwards bound and return journey, so if you could invoice me I will be happy to forward the respective moneys.

You can also rest assured that all the stuffed spouses will be covered in grey body-socks whilst outside of the environs of the carriage. I can also assure you that all living spouses are well able to manoeuvre their respective stuffed spouses without troubling your platform staff. I will also ensure that all spouses bring with them their annual taxidermy certificates for your assessment.

Thank you once again for being so accommodating.

Yours truly,

Bertha Sykes (Retired)

148 Montpelier Rd,
Brighton,
East Sussex,
BN1 2LQ.

27.07.04

Archbishop of Westminster,
Archbishop's House,
Westminster,
London,
SW1P 1QJ

Dear Archbishop,

I am writing to you because I want to know about God and Heaven and Hell and some other things. My Granny is typing this letter for me. She used to be a secretary when she was young.

Is God like a man or a woman? My Daddy says that God is like a man with a long white beard, but my Mummy says that God's just like a woman. My Granny says that it's up to me to decide what God looks like, and I don't have to just copy what my Mummy and Daddy think. Granny says that God might just as well look like a monkey or a Giraffe. I think that maybe God is half a female and half a male, but I'm not sure which would be the top and which would be the bottom. My Granny has said that that would make God a hermaphrodite. That sounds very complicated to me.

I also want to know where God lives. I know that he lives in Heaven but I would like to know where heaven is. If you had a big telescope would you be able to see heaven in the sky? Mummy and Daddy say that heaven is not here on the Earth so it must be up in the sky somewhere. If it's not up there then where else can it be?

I also don't understand where Hell is. Is it under the ground? If I got a big spade and dug a very big hole would I end up in Hell with the Devil? Also, if Heaven is such a long, long way away, how come the Devil is so close? I don't think that is very fair. I do not want to go to Hell, but if I ever end up there I will get a big spade and dig a big hole in the roof until I get back to Brighton again. I don't want to burn forever.

I would also like to know when Jesus is coming to visit us again. I would like to meet Jesus when he comes. Will he come with his Mummy and Daddy too? I think it would be very nice for lots of people if Jesus comes. I think he would like Brighton. There are lots of cafes and places to buy ice creams. He could meet my dog, Charlie.

Could you tell me if people ever come out of their graves like in the film I have seen? I do not want to be near graves at night. And can you tell me if these people are vampires?

Thank you,

Amanda Hastings (age 7).

09 August 2004

Dear Amanda,

The Cardinal thanks you for your letter to him and would like to thank your Granny for typing the letter on your behalf. Unfortunately, he is not in London for the next few days and so he has asked me to reply for him.

You ask some very important questions about God and about heaven and hell and when Jesus is going to come again. These are all very difficult problems that people have been asking for many years, and the Church has answers to all these questions, but many of them would be very difficult for you to understand. But they are questions that you are right to ask and they are questions that are asked in schools, and at our local parish churches. There are also a great many books written especially for people of your age that help you to understand who God is, and where He lives. One thing is certain, Amanda, it is very difficult to understand God because He is so big, and so clever, and we have to accept that a lot of things that we believe about him are wrapped up in a mystery that is bigger than ourselves, and anything that we can imagine.

I hope that you will not give up asking your questions, and discussing things about our faith. One thing we believe very strongly is that Jesus will come again at the end of time and He will come to reward us if we have been good and to invite us to be with Him in heaven.

With all good wishes,

Yours sincerely,

Rev. Mgr. John Arnold
<u>Vicar General</u>

Miss Amanda Hastings,
148 Montpelier Road,
Brighton
East Sussex
BN1 2LQ

148 Montpelier Rd,
Brighton,
East Sussex,
BN1 2LQ.

Richard Branson,
Virgin Atlantic Airways,
Sussex House,
High Street,
Crawley,
Sussex,
RH10 1DQ

Dear Richard,

I am writing to you with regard to what I consider to be a very serious matter. I have recently returned from a holiday with my girlfriend in the Philippines. Whilst there we decided to explore a small archipelago of islands, a number of which are uninhabited. We asked if we could be dropped off on one of these islands for an afternoon and the captain of the boat we'd hired duly obliged.

All would have been uneventful if we hadn't decided to make a small exploration inland. We had only journeyed a short distance when we heard voices. We would have gone back to the beach straight away but for the fact that we were intrigued that the conversation was being conducted in English. A short distance later, and viewed safely from the canopy of the jungle itself, we came upon a most disturbing scene.

In a clearing were three bearded Caucasian males tethered to a large iron pole. They were arguing about who was going to chew the fish bones first. Two of them had their backs to us, but the third was clearly visible and though dirty and unkempt he bore an uncanny resemblance to a certain Richard Branson. I whispered this to my girlfriend who then dropped her camera in horror. But the true horror occurred moments later when, disturbed by the noise of the camera hitting a rock on the ground, the other men turned their faces in our direction. They were Richard Bransons' too!

We ran for our lives to the beach and waited in fear until our boat arrived. Back on the mainland we rescheduled our flights and returned to England as soon as we could. We have now been back for a week, and after lengthy discussion we have decided to give you the benefit of the doubt, and allow you a chance to explain just what the hell is going on.

We presume you know all about these 'doppelgangers'. The chances of three persons being roughly identical to you being present in the same place at the same time are quite infinitesimal I think you'll agree.

So what's the story? And why were these haggard and thin facsimiles chained up on a remote faraway island? Perhaps you will tell us that they are your other quadruplet brothers. Fat chance! We checked the birth registry and there is no record other than for your own singular birth.

So, it looks like we're talking clones, doesn't it Richard? Are they kept there in case you need spare body parts? Are they just poor creatures farmed for your convenience and uses? Or, perhaps, there may be something even more sinister behind this than we have yet imagined?

My girlfriend and I eagerly await your response, but if we have not heard back within one week we will be taking this story straight to Max Clifford and through him to the World's press.

Yours faithfully,

Matthew Hardy.
Tanya Lycott-Smythe.

 Virgin Management Ltd.

Our ref: dg/050804/lfj

5th August 2004

Matthew Hardy & Tanya Lycott-Smythe
148 Montpelier Road
Brighton
East Sussex
BN1 2LQ

Dear Matthew & Tanya

Many thanks for your letter. How strange!

I certainly haven't been anywhere near the Philippines lately and I don't have any identical brothers that I know of!!!

Kind Regards

Richard Branson
Chairman
Virgin Group of Companies

(Dictated by Richard Branson and signed in his absence)

148 Montpelier Rd,
Brighton,
East Sussex,
BN1 2LQ.

General Enquiries,
Madame Tussauds,
Marylebone Road,
London.

Dear Sir or Madam,

I am writing to you on behalf of my Aunt, Mrs Winifred Nixon-McCateer. Winifred lost her husband of forty years last spring and has not really got over the loss. We are a close-knit family and we have all pulled together to help Winny, but at times she is inconsolable. She has now come up with a quite extraordinary plan, which she thinks will make her grieve much less.

Captain Philip Nixon-McCateer served in Egypt during the Second World War and stayed in that country at the close of the war where he remained for a number of years, becoming something of an Egyptologist. After his death, and according to his wishes, he was mummified and then entombed in the family vault.

Winny would like to have her husband disentombed and shipped to London. The company that mummified him in the first place would then reverse this mummification. I am reliably informed that after such a short amount of time Philip will be in very good condition.

Winny would then like Philip to be ferried to yourselves in order to have all the vital measurements taken for you to be able to create a waxwork model of him. A vital part of the mummification process involves complete disembowelling and removal of other extraneous material. So, even at room temperature you will still be able to work happily with Philip for up to four days without him becoming in any way offensive to your employees. When you have completed all the requisite measurements and preliminary modelling we will simple arrange for Philip to be collected, re-mummified and quietly replaced in the family vault.

We will, of course, provide his full military uniform for your convenience, as this is how Winny would like him to be clothed. When work is complete we would arrange to have the doppelganger Philip transported to Aunt Winifred's home.

I realise that this request may seem extraordinary to you, but Winny is convinced it will cheer her up enormously. It is for this reason that we have all supported her in attempting to make this a possibility.

Do you think that you would be able to help fulfil my Aunt's wishes? If you need any more details I would be happy to oblige, and let me say right at the outset that money is no object for us. We will pay whatever it costs.

I should be most grateful if you could get back to me with your decision.

Yours truly,

Earnest Fellowes.

MADAME
TUSSAUDS
LONDON

2nd August 2004

Earnest Fellowes
148 Montpelier Road
Brighton
East Sussex BN1 2LQ

Dear Mr Fellowes

Thank you for your letter, and sincere condolences to your aunt on her very sad loss.

We would indeed be able to make a wax figure of Captain Nixon-McCateer. However, if you are happy to supply photographs, we would be able to create the Captain's likeness without having to have his mummified body dis-emtombed & shipped to our Studios. This would be one option, and we would be able to create a figure for £95,000.

If this is not possible, we would then need to make other arrangements and, if indeed it came to taking measurements from the body, creating a wax figure would cost in the region of £250,000.

In either case, we would require a 50% deposit before proceeding with the commission.

I look forward to hearing from you.

With very best wishes

General Enquiries Department
Madame Tussauds London

FRENCH'S ZOO

148 Montpelier Rd, Brighton, East Sussex, BN1 2LQ

Isles of Scilly Tourist Information,
The Old Wesleyan Chapel,
St Mary's Well Lane,
Isles of Scilly,
Cornwall,
TR21 0H2

Dear Sir or Madam,

I am writing to you as the artistic director of French's Zoo, based here in Brighton. We believe that French's is the world's first make-believe zoo, and we are actively seeking to promote French's after our grand opening during May as part of the Brighton Festival.

Would you be prepared to stock some of our make-believe brochures? If you have the room we can also provide a make-believe colour cardboard showcase for the aforementioned brochures. We would also like to discuss with you your willingness to take bookings for us at your offices. Perhaps you have some pertinent information that you could send to us regarding this matter.

We really feel that French's offers something quite unique to Brighton, and we all hope that our little make-believe zoo can find the funding to continue well into the future. A number of us have put in considerable time and effort into getting French's up and running, and then of course there are the make-believe animals to consider. We have make-believe giraffes, make-believe rhinoceroses, make-believe lions and tigers, make-believe iguanas, make-believe dolphins and whales, make-believe kangaroos, make-believe parrots – we've even got a make-believe unicorn! Not many 'real' zoos could boast of having one of those!

Of course one of the greatest benefits of a make-believe zoo is that we do not have our animals chained up or imprisoned in any way. This means that, with a little imagination, children visiting our zoo are able to get right up close to creatures that, in the real world, would prove an extreme danger or threat. Our animals are only as fearful as the children allow them to be.

I hope that the above information is of assistance to you, and I look forward to hearing back from you in due course.

Yours truly,

Guy Piran

Aberdeen
and Grampian
TOURIST BOARD

16 August 2004
01224 288818
mwearmouth@agtb.oprg
cus-co/mmw/hir

Mr G Piran
FRENCH'S ZOO
148 Montpelier Road
BRIGHTON
East Sussex
BN1 2LQ

Dear Mr Piran

Thank you for your recent letter and please accept my apologies for the delay in replying.

Your *make-believe* zoo certainly sounds like a wonderful idea and we would be delighted to stock some of your brochures - say 50 to begin with. Unfortunately we are limited for space so we shall be unable to display your leaflets in their colour cardboard showcase.

Please accept my best wishes for success in your venture.

Yours sincerely

Margaret M Wearmouth
Customer Services Manager

FRENCH'S ZOO

148 Montpelier Rd, Brighton, East Sussex, BN1 2LQ

Margaret M Wearmouth,
Customer services Manager,
Exchange House,
26/28 Exchange Street,
Aberdeen,
AB11 6PH
Scotland.

Dear Margaret,

Thank you so much for responding to my earlier correspondence and for taking such an interest in our little make-believe zoo. We all think it's a wonderful idea and we're pleased to know that you think so too.

Please find enclosed 50 make-believe brochures along with three of our very best make-believe display units. In your letter you say you are 'limited in space' but as you can now see our display units take up no more room than our make-believe brochures.

In addition please find enclosed three miniature make-believe unicorns. Their names are Mandy, Edgar and Tulip. In recent conversation they have all expressed an interest in finding pastures new, and that is why we have sent them up to the delightful country of Scotland.

I can assure you that they are all extremely well educated and well versed in Scottish folklore and history. I hope they are an asset to your Tourist Board Offices. They will also keep any mischievous leprechauns well away from your environs, as well as granting each member of your staff a wish on the first of every month.

Thank you once again for wishing us success in our venture.

Yours truly,

Guy Piran.

148 Montpelier Rd,
Brighton,
East Sussex,
BN1 2LQ.

Head Keeper,
Newquay Zoo,
Trenance Gardens,
Newquay,
Cornwall,
TR7 2LZ.

Dear Sir/Madam,

I am writing to you in the first instance as I feel that you may be more sympathetic to my cause than London Zoo. I am a writer, and at present I am coming to the end of a two-year project evaluating instances of platonic love between the animal kingdom and that of human beings. During this time I have conducted lengthy experiments between myself and any number of different animals.

I started my experiments with our family's two pet poodles but soon realised that any experimentation would not really stand up to close scientific scrutiny due to my already lengthy relationship with these particular beasts.

I therefore moved on to wilder creatures such as squirrels and pigeons and soon had a couple of very useful encounters with a badger. After that I turned my attention to herbivores of all varieties (always with the express permission of their owners!).

A good friend of mine in publishing thinks that I should conclude my analysis with a large wild creature such as a lion, and that is why I am writing to you in this instance. Would it be possible to rent one of your lions for a weekend? I can assure you that your lion would be treated with the greatest respect and I would lay-in whatever food was required. Further to this I would hire a Malaysian lion-tamer called Wenai Pongscripian, who has a great deal of experience with large cats. I am willing to pay whatever price is necessary and would further consider making a donation to your park on top of this fee.

I hope that you consider my request.

Yours truly,

Guy Piran.

**Zoological Gardens and British
Wildlife Rescue Centre**

9th August 2004

Dear Mr Piran

I feel we are something of kindred spirits as I have a firm and spiritual belief that some people have the ability to have deep and meaningful and in some cases telepathic relationships with their animals. I consider myself very fortunate to work in a zoo where I'm occasionally able to fondle certain animals, particularly my primates.

In answer to your query regarding our lions Ronnie and Connie, I feel unable to help you as they are already in an established relationship which is far from platonic. Indeed the sexual side of their relationship shows no inhibitions, as the number of complaints which my office receives about their lovemaking will testify (mostly neighbours complaining about the roaring).

I should make you aware also that in order to house large carnivores such as lions you would need a dangerous wild animals act licence for which you would need to be thoroughly vetted by your local authority. This is to safeguard any dangerous animal coming into the possession of people unable to house them suitably and whose motives may be dubious such as deviants and the mentally ill.

Therefore I deeply regret that we are unable to help you in this matter.

Best wishes

Yours sincerely

Stewart Muir

Stewart Muir
Assistant Director

Newquay Zoo, Trenance Gardens,
Newquay, Cornwall TR7 2LZ
Tel 01637 873342
Fax 01637 851318
Email info@newquayzoo.org.uk
www.newquayzoo.org.uk

148 Montpelier Rd,
Brighton,
East Sussex,
BN1 2LQ.

Dodds Auctioneers,
9 Chester Street,
Mold,
Flintshire,
CH7 1EG

Dear Sir or Madam,

I am writing to ask your advice regarding an antique that I have in my possession. The antique in question is my Great Grandfather, Percival Fothergill II.

Percival has been kept in my family since he was stuffed in 1871, and comes in a large glass presentation case. The case itself is mounted on a large mahogany plinth, which is of a sturdy construct. Percival is dressed in his hunting breeches and tweeds, and is positioned standing atop a realistic-looking rocky outcrop. At his feet lie stuffed pheasants and grouse, and by his side stands his trusty hunting hound, Growler.

Although the birds are a little moth-eaten and, shall we say, a little past their sell-by date, both Percival and Growler are in pretty much immaculate condition. Both have recently been inspected by a respected taxidermist and given a clean bill of health, as it were.

Unfortunately due to unforeseen circumstances our family has had to undergo a certain amount of downsizing. This has meant that we have had to move into much less spacious accommodation. In our previous property we had ample room to accommodate Percival (we had him positioned on the mezzanine level in the hallway), but we simply do not have room for him in our two-bedroom terrace house in Brighton. As it turns out we would also be in contravention of our leasehold agreement. That is why, sadly, we feel we have to let Percival go.

Do you think there would be interest in the auction market for Percival and his animal entourage? I am sure that you are not requested to auction Great Grandfather's very often – especially ones that are stuffed! However, I can assure you that there is nothing unseemly about Percival whatsoever. On the contrary, the whole package is very tastefully presented and certainly very eye-catching. It is also, of course, an antique.

My family hope that Percival might, perhaps, appeal to the overseas market, especially that of the USA. We can provide ample amounts of documents detailing Percival's provenance. In addition to this, we can also include in any package, a calf-bound photographic album featuring over 100 prints of Percival when he was alive.

If you so wish I would be more than happy to send you photographs of Percival in his presentation case, along with some documents detailing his provenance. If, however, you would rather see him in person, as it were, then I can make arrangements to have Percival transported to your auction rooms for further detailed assessment.

I would be most grateful if you could get back to me on this as soon as possible as Percival is proving to be quite an encumbrance in our new home.

Yours truly,

Hilda Fothergill-Percy.

DODDS

ESTATE AGENTS
AUCTIONEERS
SURVEYORS
VALUERS

PLEASE REPLY TO
MOLD OFFICE - 01352 752552

www.door-key.com
e-mail:dodds@door-key.com

PARTNERS: JOHN HUGHES, ANAEA, AIBA, FPCS.
ANTHONY H. PARRY, AIBA, FPCS, FNAVA. CHRIS J. MURPHY, FNAEA.
ASSOCIATES: PEARL PARRY, JOY ROBERTS, ANAEA.
MARGARET TAYLOR, ANAEA. MARK ESPLEY, BA(HONS).
MARIA JONES, ANAEA. LYNNE EVANS

Our Ref: ourref AHP / MWE

29th July 2004.

Ms H. Fothergill-Percy,
148, Montpelier Road,
Brighton,
East Sussex, BN1 2LQ

Dear Ms Fothergill-Percy,

Re : Your Great Grandfather, Percival Fothergill II (Deceased) !

Many thanks for your undated letter received this morning.

We must admit that we did have to read the letter several times, as to say the least we have never been asked to sell anyone's great grandfather before.

In the past we have sold many unusual items but never a "Percival". The nearest we have had was a Grandfather Clock in which a previous owner had concealed the body of his wife, having murdered her!

We are sure that there would be an interest in the auction market for Percival and his animal entourage. With the advent of the internet worldwide publicity is within reach.

We do have the World Record for selling a Welsh Dresser, but we are intrigued to know why you chose us to be entrusted with Percival ? . Have you seen us featured on television in the programmes, "Bargain Hunt" or "Flog It" .

Please let us have a photograph and your telephone number in order that we may be of assistance to you in finding Percival a new home!

Yours sincerely,

ANTHONY H. PARRY, F.N.A.V.A,., F.N.A.E.A., F.P.C.S.,
PARTNER
DODDS PROPERTY WORLD.

PROPERTY SALES: 17 Grosvenor Street, CHESTER, Cheshire CH1 2DD (01244) 348737, Fax: 400545: 9 Chester St., MOLD, Flintshire, CH7 1EG (01352) 752552, Fax 752542:
The Cross, BUCKLEY, Flintshire, CH7 2JL (01244) 550511, Fax 547622: 20 Chester Rd West, SHOTTON, Deeside, Flintshire, CH5 1BX (01244) 813442, Fax 831414: St Peter's
Sq. RUTHIN Denbighshire LL15 1DH (01824) 703936, Fax 702615 : High St, BALA, Gwynedd LL23 7AG (01678) 520495 Fax: 520663 : 25 Vale St, DENBIGH, Denbighshire
LL16 3AH (01745) 812685 Fax: 812830: SURVEY SERVICE, The Cross BUCKLEY, Flintshire CH7 2JL (01244) 547622 (Phone/Fax): VICTORIA AUCTION GALLERIES, MOLD,
Flintshire, CH7 1EG (01352) 755705, Fax 752542 : COMMERCIAL 17 Grosvenor St, CHESTER, Cheshire CH1 2DD (01244) 348737, Fax 400545.
www.door-key.com e-mail:dodds@door-key.com

148 Montpelier Rd,
Brighton,
East Sussex,
BN1 2LQ.

Cambridge University Press,
The Edinburgh Building,
Shaftesbury Road,
Cambridge,
CB2 2RU

Dear Sir or Madam,

I am writing to you with joy and untrammeled excitation. I have just completed my first book and I know that it's a sure-fire winner. Nobody in the history of publishing has ever published a book quite like this one, and that's why I know that it's going to be a runaway success. When this book's published it will act as a benchmark for all future books to do with the subject. I also do not doubt that it will spawn many imitators - but they'll only ever come in second if you do the wise thing and take this book on.

My book is called 'Sex Tool Items For Free' (S.T.I.F.F.) and is the culmination of many months of research and sometimes fevered application. I have left no stone unturned in my tireless attempts to map the very boundaries of general household and garden implementation, and I can now certainly assure you that this book is extremely encyclopedic in breadth and vision.

It is also a book for the common man. All the items that I explore are all things that people will normally have lying around the house; and in terms of the garden equipment that I have explored, these are all relatively cheap items to acquire, even if the reader doesn't have a garden!

A brief random selection of items which I have discovered how to use as sex tools includes, a Fairy Liquid bottle, a Hoover (upright model), sticky-backed plastic, a monkey wrench, a kitchen blender, a washing machine, an electric extension lead (12 metres), the complete works of William Shakespeare, the complete works of Charles Dickens, a jar of pickled onions, a garden trowel, a garden rake, a hose-pipe, one dining table + 2 chairs, a pair of walking boots, a screw-in light-bulb (100 watts), and a typical-sized family hamster cage (with wheel!).

As you can see from the above the sky's the limit once you get going, but I should point out that not all of my applications are entirely obvious. In fact the best 'tools', can sometimes be used in any number of different ways that only a devotee like me could have dreamt up in the first place. That's why this book is unique: Joe Bloggs could probably think of a couple of sexual applications for a Fairy Liquid bottle if pushed, but I bet he'd never come up with over a hundred! And I've got five whole pages devoted to William Shakespeare alone. How's that for dedication and devotion?

I know that this is definitely going to be a book that requires photographs and/or annotated sketches, and to that end I have laboured to come up with some sketches and photographs of my own. I will admit that I'm no David Bailey or, for that matter, much of a Rembrandt, but I'm sure they'll give your creative department a really good idea about what I was aiming at.

I really think that this is a jaw-opening book and that you will not want to let this opportunity pass you by. I have everything parceled-up and ready to pop in the post, so all you've got to do is get in touch.

I very much look forward to hearing from you soon.

Yours truly,

Arthur Smithkins

P.S. Could you please respond by letter? My wife and I are going through something of a messy divorce at the moment and I am having to live in Bed and Breakfast's. I am, however, able to pick up my post once a week!

CAMBRIDGE
UNIVERSITY PRESS

The Edinburgh Building
Shaftesbury Road
Cambridge CB2 2RU, UK

www.cambridge.org

Telephone +44 (0)1223 325184
Fax +44 (0)1223 325701
Email sbourne@cambridge.org

Mr A Smithkins
148 Montpelier Road
Brighton
East Sussex BN1 2LQ

3 August 2004

Dear Mr Smithkins

In response to your vibrant letter received on 29 July, I'm afraid I must be disappointingly dull by saying that your research is not the kind of material we would be expected to publish here at Cambridge University Press, so I fear that we would not be successful in enabling your book to reach its full potential. Intriguing though the content may be, I must, regrettably, decline.

Yours sincerely

PS   I confess to being a little bothered about the precise application of the kitchen blender …

The Sobriety Society

148 Montpelier Road, Brighton, East Sussex, BN1 2LQ.

Claridge's Restaurant,
Claridge's,
Brock Street,
London,
W1A 2JQ

Dear Sir or Madam,

I am writing to you as the chairman of the Sobriety Society. After much deliberation and consultation we have decided that our 100th anniversary merits a commemorative occasion. We would therefore like to hire out your restaurant for the evening, and I am writing to you in this instance to ask if this would be possible?

There would be exactly 44 'SS' members attending any such event, and though we realise that this number will fall well short of your normal amount of covers, we wish to have the restaurant entirely to ourselves. We imagine that there would be a severe conflict of interest occurring otherwise. Let me explain in more detail.

The Sobriety Society was started in 1903 by the Right Reverend Ernest Maplin after his return from twenty years of missionary work in the Congo. He started it not only as a response to the heathen excess he had been subject to witnessing in Africa, but also to what he saw as the libertine attitude of late Victorian England. Within months of its inception he had an enthusiastic and devoted following. All of these founding fathers of our society renounced all worldly vices and any other sins of the flesh.

To this day we adhere to the strict guidelines set down by our founding father. It was, then, with some difficulty that we finally decided upon a restaurant commemorative meal. This meal is to be in no way a 'celebratory' meal whatsoever - that would go against all the principles that we stand for today and that the Right Reverend Ernerst Maplin instigated. That is why, for example, we certainly would not wish for normal restaurant clientele to be present at the same time as ourselves.

Further to this, we will require that you certainly 'tone-down' your restaurant for any such occasion. If there is an open bar area where alcoholic beverages are contained we would require that this be closed off to view, or all of the aforementioned beverages removed for the entirety of our stay at the restaurant. It goes without saying that none of our members will require anything more to drink than still mineral water.

We also hope that you can provide us with a scaled-down version of your usual menu. We will require a simple soup for starters, followed by a choice of two meats with accompanying vegetables. Any sweets on offer should be simple and wholesome (this excludes ice creams, fritters, cakes, etc).

With respect to your serving staff, we will require them to address all members of our party as 'sir' or 'madam' throughout the evening. On no account should they engage or attempt to engage in 'small-talk' or idle chatter with any of our members. We also require that they do not in any way indicate mirth or jollity - and this includes smiling! Our members are not accustomed to being smiled at whatsoever.

Our 100th anniversary falls on the 18th December and we would require the use of your restaurant on a weekday evening of the week following. We will, of course, be prepared to compensate you for the shortfall in covers on this particular evening.

I hope to hear from you soon.

Yours truly,

Timothy Horace Smythe

Mr. Timothy Horace Smythe
The Sobriety Society
148 Montpelier Road
Brighton
EAST SUSSEX BN1 2LQ

5th August 2004

Thank you for your letters to *Pétrus* and *Gordon Ramsay at Claridge's*.

I don't think that we are going to be able to accommodate your 100th anniversary evening as your requirements are the very antithesis of what we offer and I am afraid all our staff are encouraged to smile at all times. Perhaps you will be kind enough to excuse us on this occasion.

With kind regards,

Yours sincerely,

Chris Hutcheson
CEO for Gordon Ramsay Holdings

GORDON RAMSAY HOLDINGS LIMITED

1 CATHERINE PLACE
LONDON SW1E 6DX
TEL 020 7592 1360
FAX 020 7592 1366

REGISTERED NO. 3457208
ENGLAND

The Sobriety Society

148 Montpelier Road, Brighton, East Sussex, BN1 2LQ.

Chris Hutcheson Esq,
Gordon Ramsay Holdings Limited,
1 Catherine Place,
London,
SW1E 6DX

Dear Sir,

I address this letter to you in the firm knowledge that it will be 'screened' from the 'celebrity' cook that you are employed by. When I recently wrote to both Petrus and Claridge's I was sourcing the use of the restaurants for the above society. In simple terms I requested that food be simplified on that particular evening, symbols of excess such as alcohol be excluded from view, and that serving staff refrain from any customary small-talk and fraternisation with Sobriety Society members.

You write back as if offended by my proposals. You say that our requirements are the 'very antithesis of what we offer'. Perhaps you might like to explain what is antithetical about a restaurant providing simple, wholesome food, and providing waiting staff that are civil and orderly? I would have thought that that would be what any half-decent restaurant worth its salt would aspire towards.

To provide proof that the above restaurants do in fact exist, I enclose copies of letters from Pied a Terre and Brasserie St Quentin who are more than happy to accommodate our society's wishes.

I don't expect to hear back from Gordon Ramsay himself – I'm sure he's far too busy making a fool of himself on terrestrial television!

Yours faithfully,

Timothy Horace Smythe

Mr. Timothy Horace Smythe
The Sobriety Society
148 Montpelier Road
Brighton
East Sussex BN1 2LQ

10th August 2004

Dear Mr. Smythe,

Thank you very much for your letter and its enclosures.

I am very pleased that you have found two restaurants that can accommodate your members and I am only sorry that we were not able to be of service to your Society on this occasion.

Yours sincerely,

Chris Hutcheson
CEO
Gordon Ramsay Holdings

GORDON RAMSAY HOLDINGS LIMITED

1 CATHERINE PLACE
LONDON SW1E 6DX
TEL 020 7592 1360
FAX 020 7592 1366

REGISTERED NO. 3457208
ENGLAND

148 Montpelier Rd,
Brighton,
East Sussex,
BN1 2LQ.

Vanish Customer Care,
PO Box 118,
Clevedon,
BS21 7ZH

Dear Vanish,

I am writing to you because I find myself in something of a predicament. I am in possession of some bed linen, most of which is covered with a large amount of bloodstains. I have tried just about everything under the sun to get this blood out, including hand-wringing, hot washes, and copious amounts of soaking. Nothing seems to shift the stuff - not even the smallest of spots. Is there anything that you could suggest that I have not yet tried? Perhaps, you know of a product that can shift the dirtiest of stains, or, indeed, you manufacture one yourself?

My husband keeps telling me that I should go out and buy some replacement linen and stop worrying about the old stuff, but I'm afraid I've now got something of a fixation about the matter and I would dearly like to redeem the existant linen.

I hope you can write back to me with some sound advice and, perhaps, recommendations as to what I should do in the future.

Yours sincerely,

Glenda McBeth.

RECKITT BENCKISER

Ms G McBeth
148 Montpelier Road
BRIGHTON
BN1 2LQ

1244100

03 August 2004

Dear Ms McBeth

Thank you for your recent letter, regarding Vanish and the removal of blood stains.

Vanish has been designed to remove normal household stains. However, stain removal performance is influenced by many factors including stain type, age, intensity, fabric type, and previous treatments (i.e. washing or ironing can set a stain, as can use of other stain removal treatments).

Vanish is effective on a very wide range of stains but occasionally, repeat treatments may be necessary. Vanish Oxi Action has proven to be very successful in removing oxidizable stains, e.g. fruit juices, red wine, tea, coffee, water based ink, coke, grass and mud. These are accepted as some of the toughest household stains to remove. Other stains, such as butter, olive oil and dairy products, may be more effectively removed by one of our other products, e.g. Vanish Action Ball, Vanish Pre Wash Spray, Vanish Gel or Vanish In Wash Liquid.

I hope this information is of some assistance to you.

Yours sincerely

Melisa Bryant
Consumer Services Department

Castles In The Sky Incorporated

148 Montpelier Road, Brighton, East Sussex, BN1 2LQ.

Arun District Council,
Arun Civic Centre,
Maltravers Rd,
Littlehampton,
West Sussex,
BN17 5LF

Dear Sir or Madam,

I am writing to you as the head of 'Castles in the Sky Incorporated'. I started the firm back in 1992 and since then I have been responsible for a number of erections in the United Kingdom and elsewhere in the world. I think that I can safely say that I run a completely unique company, cornering a market which no-one else seems to realise the potential of at present.

I have recently been approached by a Mr Eric Simpson of Oxford Rd, Littlehampton, who wishes for my company to erect a castle in the sky directly above his premises in the aforementioned Oxford Rd. He has specified that he wishes this castle to be the biggest of its kind, and I have assured Mr Simpson that my team of architects will, in time, come up with a castle in the sky the like of which hasn't even been dreamt of before. It has always been my personal priority to ensure complete customer satisfaction on a money-back guarantee, and to this day I have never had an unsatisfied customer .

I am writing to you as a courtesy in order to inform you that my company is shortly to commence work on Mr Simpson's very own castle in the sky. As I'm sure you will understand, planning permission for the erection of such edifices is never needed due to the ephemeral and lightweight nature of these constructions. However, I still feel that any city council still has the right to be made aware of construction, however imagined, taking place within its environs.

I can assure you that during the construction process my company will in no way cause any disruption at all either in or around Littlehampton, and we hope to have Mr Simpson's castle completed early in 2005.

If for whatever reason you wish to raise any further questions with me over my erection then please to not hesitate to contact me at the above address.

Yours truly,

Harry Threwlss, M.A.

A R U N
DISTRICT COUNCIL

Arun District Council
Arun Civic Centre
Maltravers Road
Littlehampton
West Sussex
BN17 5LF

Tel: (01903) 737500

Fax: (01903) 716019
DX: 57406
Minicom: (01903) 732765

e-mail: planning@arun.gov.uk

H Threwliss Esq MA
Castles in the Sky Incorporated
148 Montpelier Road
BRIGHTON
East Sussex
BN1 2LQ

24 August 2004

Please ask for:
Keith Wheway
Principal Planner
Tel: (01903) 737794

Your Ref:

Our Ref: KW/jtg

Dear Mr Threwliss

Thank you for your letter of 29 July 2004.

I am not convinced that this structure does not need planning permission, and of course it would be open to you to submit an application for a Certificate of Lawfulness of purposed use, in order that the Authority can make a formal decision on this matter. I attach a set of forms for your use.

I hope this information is of assistance to you.

Yours sincerely

Keith Wheway
Principal Planner (Development Control)

Enc

51

East Sussex Coven of Witches

148 Montpelier Road, Brighton, East Sussex, BN1 2LQ.

Which? Ltd,
2 Marylebone Rd,
London,
NW1 4DF

Dear Sir or Madam,

I am writing to you as the High Priestess of the East Sussex Coven of Witches. I have been in this position for a number of years now and hold authority over 130 witches in the magic triangle covered by the three points of Brighton, Lewes and Eastbourne.

At one of our regular get-togethers what has often been a recurrent problem resurfaced yet again - namely, how do you know which is the right witch to go for in any particular instance. For example, the last thing you want to do if you're thinking of having a love-charm cast over an intended lover, is to seek the help and assistance of a black witch. Conversely, a white witch is going to be little use to you if you need to do away with some of your arch-enemies.

The above, of course, are extreme examples. As any witch will tell you, there is an enormous spectrum of grey between these two polar opposites. This grey zone is where the majority of witchcraft is practiced and consequently where the majority if witching assistance is sought.

What my coven and I are writing to suggest is that, with our assistance, the Which magazine publishes a clear and easy-to-understand catalogue of witchcraft practitioners and their relative positions on the all-important grey-scale. We envisage that using various tones of grey the general public will be able to match up with a practitioner that most suits their individual purposes and requirements.

Some of our members in the East Sussex Coven of Witches, including myself, being long-standing servants of the sorceric community , we would also be in a position to come up with a star system to identify which of the individual practitioners listed gets the best results for their clients. This would, we think, be entirely in keeping with the traditional format used by the Which Magazine to distinguish, for example, between the best and the worst washing machines.

I'm sure that this letter will raise further questions that you would like answered, so please do not hesitate to contact me at the above address. I really think that if Which Magazine were to work with us on this 'witchcraft in the community' report it would be of great use not just to all the witches out there but also the often misinformed and undiscerning public.

I look forward to hearing from you in due course.

Yours truly,

Tabitha Fourpaws

WHICH❓

Castlemead
Gascoyne Way
Hertford X
SG14 1LH
0845 307 4000
Fax 0845 307 4001
email which@which.net
http://www.which.co.uk/

305595806K
Ms Tabitha Fourpaws
148 Montpellier Road
BRIGHTON
BN1 2LQ

6 August, 2004

Dear Ms Fourpaws

WHEADC/08/FOU/600/7.2/W

While we always appreciate suggestions for future articles, we do however have to draw a line at what we provide information on. Our reports focus on widely purchased consumer goods, and the services most needed by consumers, so in all honesty, I am going to have to say your suggestion is not something we would generally do, as it is more of a specified subject.

I really hope that you understand our position on this matter.

Yours sincerely

Mark Hale
Customer Services

EAST SUSSEX PYGMY APPRECIATION SOCIETY

148 Montpelier Road, Brighton, East Sussex, BN1 2LQ.

The Manager,
Chelsea Football Club,
Stamford Bridge,
Fulham Rd,
London,
SW6 1HS

Dear Sir,

I am writing to you as the acting head of the East Sussex Pygmy Appreciation Society, based here in Brighton. People are often surprised to know just how much pygmy appreciation there is out there, and I can proudly inform you that I have just signed up our 100th member. Indeed, it has been this particular new member (the Right Reverend Ian Blackwell) who has come up with the idea which I am now going to put to you.

Would it be at all feasible to hire out Chelsea Football team for a match against the Freewheeling Pygmies. The Freewheeling Pygmies are an international football team made up of the best pygmy football stars that the world has to offer. The Freewheeling Pygmies are worldbeaters, and that's why they'd like to take on Chelsea Football team.

Other than the size of the football, the length and breadth of the pitch, and the height and width of the goal there would be no significant difference between 'pygmy' football and that practiced by your regular team members. One allowance that is always requested, however, is that unlike football for the vertically unchallenged, the pygmy side are allowed to run between the legs of their opponents. We have found in the past that this does somewhat level the playing field, and, for example, redress the obvious advantage that other teams can have in terms of, say, heading the ball.

If you could get back to me with any queries that you may have, and as to the very possibility of hiring your football team in the first place, then I would be most grateful.

Yours truly,

Oliver Sochs (BSE)

CHELSEA FOOTBALL CLUB

STAMFORD BRIDGE
LONDON SW6 1HS

Phone: 00 44 (020) 7385 5545
Fax: 00 44 (020) 7381 4831
Website: www.chelseafc.com

Jm/jw

29th July 2004

O SOCHS ESQ
East Sussex Pygmy Appreciation Society
148 Montpelier Road
BRIGHTON
East Sussex BN1 2LQ

Dear Oliver,

Thank you for your recent letter regarding the possibility of Chelsea taking part in a friendly match against the Freewheeling Pygmies.

Unfortunately with the season starting in less than three weeks we are not looking for any friendly matches.

Sorry we are unable to help with your request on this occasion.

With best wishes.

Yours sincerely,

Jose Mourinho
Manager

CLUB SPONSOR

SPORTSWEAR SPONSOR

148 Montpelier Rd,
Brighton,
East Sussex,
BN1 2LQ.

Lake District National Park Authority,
Murley Moss,
Oxenholme Rd,
Kendal,
Cumbria,
LA9 7RL

Dear Sir or Madam,

My name is Derick Pringle and I used to be a pig farmer near Goole. Now I am an astronaut and I run my own space company. Some people laugh when I tell them of my farming history, but if it hadn't been for those pigs - and more importantly the stuff that comes out of them - then I would never have been in a position to fly in the first place.

I have now completed the final modifications to my latest spacecraft, which is powered using a combination of liquid nitrogen, hydrochloric acid, and methane (pig shit!). I am hoping to send myself into the stratosphere sometime on or around September 13th 2004. I have a specially adapted 2CV van which doubles as transporter and launch pad for my rocket.

Would it be possible to make use of a little bit of the Lake District National Park to facilitate my journey into space? If this is feasible could I ask that the designated area be as high up as possible? It's obvious really, but nevertheless worth pointing out, that the higher up I am on take-off, the less distance I have to travel in order to break out of the Earth's atmosphere. Sometimes the odd 1000ft is crucial.

My wife will be accompanying me to your park, and she will clear up after I have departed (extinguishing fires, removal of metal fragments, rubberwear, crockery, etc). She will then be setting off in the 2CV on a journey down to the Sierra Nevada in central Spain where I am hoping to land some 72 hours later.

I bet you don't get requests like this every day, but I do hope you can find a way of accommodating me. I can assure you that you would get some very good publicity for your national park (when I come back to Earth, Radio Goole have promised to interview me on their breakfast programme!).

I very much look forward to hearing back from you soon.

Yours truly,

Derick Pringle. O.B.B.O.

Lake District
National Park Authority

Mr Derick Pringle O.B.B.O
148 Montpelier Road
Brighton
East Sussex
BN1 2LQ

Murley Moss, Oxenholme Road
Kendal, Cumbria LA9 7RL

Telephone:	*(01539) 724555*
Fax:	*(01539) 740822*
Minicom:	*(01539) 731263*
Internet:	hq@lake-district.gov.uk
Website	www.lake-district.gov.uk
	BobCartwright@lake-district.gov.uk

Direct Dial No : 01539 792679

Our Ref: CMT/RC/ean

Your Ref:

Date: 9 August, 2004

Dear Mr Pringle

SPACE LAUNCH FROM THE LAKE DISTRICT

Thank you for your undated letter received 29 July 2004. I greatly enjoyed reading about your proposed exploits and wish you every success with your venture.

There is no reason in principle why you shouldn't use "a little bit of the Lake District" to facilitate your journey into space This is a living and working environment and all sorts of activities take place provided that they do not undermine the special qualities of the Lake District. People particularly value the opportunity for quiet enjoyment, for example, so you may need to provide some reassurance that your craft will take off fairly quietly.

You are clearly looking for a launch pad that is as high as possible. Our highest summit is just over 3,200 feet but there is no access to it by 2CV van.

I suspect that the highest pass accessible by vehicle would be the Newlands Pass above Buttermere. The key issue, of course, is that you will need landowners' consent to launch. Very little of the Lake District is owned by the National Park Authority but we do know who owns most of the land. Once you have decided on a particular launch site please contact me again and I may be able to advise you on who to speak to if you have not already been able to find that information.

Turning to your final paragraph, you are quite right that we do not get requests like this every day but your sense of optimism and adventure is absolutely in the spirit of the first National Park pioneers and even some of the people who work in this organisation.

Best wishes

Yours sincerely

BOB CARTWRIGHT
CORPORATE OPERATIONS DIRECTOR
Cc ED

2004 celebrates 50 years of service by
Voluntary Wardens to the National Park

Paul Tiplady BA, MA, MSc, MRTPI, MLI
National Park Officer

A member of the Association of National Park Authorities

A member of the Federation of Nature and National Parks of Europe

INVESTOR IN PEOPLE

148 Montpelier Rd,
Brighton,
East Sussex,
BN1 2LQ.

Embassy of Switzerland,
16-18 Montagu Place,
London,
W1H 2BQ

Dear Switzerland,

I love Switzerland! I adore all your big uplifting mountains that are often covered in supple snow. I relish your chocolate with its dark, rich purity - a chocolate that clings to the innards of the mouth like a limpet to a rocky shoreline, before slithering down the throat like a lost sheep in an alpine meadow.

I watch my clock tick-toc in that eternal endless rhythm. Tick-toc, tick-toc. Never flinching, never moody - always serving its master as a good slave should. Never hurried, never slow. Just tick-toc, tick-toc, tick-toc, tick-toc, until, without fail, and on the hour, a little head pops out and spews forth music in its beautiful birdy ejaculation. That's Swiss clock-making for you! It's the best in the world!

Sometimes I wish the whole world was Switzerland - at peace with itself and wearing funny clogs. Not interested in futile wars but happy with the Shnaps and the Lederhosen. I love Switzerland so much that I made my own Lederhosen out of used car tyres. I smell oily but I feel Swiss all over - sometimes for hours on end, even in bed!!

I want to come to Switzerland and give my love to the people. I want to hold them in my arms and yodel with my tongue. Then afterwards we can sup the limpid beer with saurkraut and sausage. This will fill me to the brim with excitement and trembling - not to mention the 'pumps'.

Can I come? Will I be welcome in my Dunlop lederhosen? Will birds twitter and tweet in the soft mountain breeze? Please tell me it can and will be so.

Yours truly,

Guy Philips,

SWISS EMBASSY
SCHWEIZERISCHE BOTSCHAFT
AMBASSADE DE SUISSE
AMBASCIATA DI SVIZZERA
AMBASSADA SVIZRA

LONDON

Ref.: 641.02POM

London W1H 2BQ, **30 July, 2004**
16-18 Montagu Place
Tel.:   (020) 7616 6000
Fax.:   (020) 7724 7001
E-mail: swissembassy@lon.rep.admin.ch

Mr Guy Philips
148 Montpelier Road
Brighton
BN1 2LQ

Dear Mr Philips

Thank you very much for your letter with the lovely poetic description of my country. I hope that you can fulfil your dream of visiting Switzerland which indeed has beautiful scenery. In the meantime please accept the enclosed souvenir items.

Should you wish to find out more about Swiss tourism please contact:

Switzerland Travel Centre
Swiss Centre
Swiss Court
London W1V 8EE
Tel: 020 7292 1550

Yours sincerely

U. Hunn
Consul General

Encs

59

148 Montpelier Rd,
Brighton,
East Sussex,
United Kingdom,
BN1 2LQ.

Leeds College of Music,
3 Quarry Hill,
Leeds,
LS2 7PD

Dear Sir or Madam,

I am writing to you concerning my late father's last will and testament. It is apparent that he has bequeathed to you an item which I think is of considerable value, both in financial and historic terms. The item concerned is a crafted oak presentation case containing the paired testicles of twelve 18th Century Italian Castrati. These aforementioned items are each seated on velvet cushioning and separated into individual compartments.

Along with the presentation case are a number of documents and letters that give accurate provenance as to the individual testicles contained therein. There are only two pairs that appear to have no documentary proof as to their origin, but they are still individually named and inscribed. Presumably with a little detective work you would be able to verify their status as well?

I am entirely sure that you will not have been made a bequest of this nature ever before. I have been in touch with both Christy's and Sotheby's and they have never come across anything of this nature themselves.

As executor of my father's estate it is my duty to offer the gift to you. If, however, you do not wish to accept this gift, a secondary clause in the will allows for our family to put the items up for auction. If you are to accept this bequest it must be made plain that the items must remain in perpetuity with the Leeds College of Music, and not be tendered for sale or auction by yourselves at any later date.

I should be most grateful if you could reply to this letter as soon as possible.

Yours truly,

Charles McCabe

Leeds College of Music

3 Quarry Hill
Leeds LS2 7PD
Telephone 0113 222 3400
Fax 0113 243 8798
E-mail enquiries@lcm.ac.uk
www.lcm.ac.uk

17 August 2004

Principal
David Hoult
MusB MPhil GRSM ARMCM FRNCM

Mr Charles McCabe
148 Montpelier Road
Brighton
East Sussex
BN1 2LQ

Leeds
College of
Music

Dear Mr McCabe

Thank you for your letter informing the College of the unusual bequest contained within your late father's last will and testament.

I have considered your letter very carefully, and have consulted with relevant colleagues regarding this response. Whilst we are honoured to have been remembered in this way by your late father, I regret that we are not able to accept this generous bequest. You are therefore at liberty to dispose of these articles in accordance with the secondary provisions in the will.

On the other hand, I believe that if sautéed in a little butter or olive oil over a gentle flame, together with a small amount of sour cream, Worcestershire sauce and a pinch of nutmeg, and garnished with a spring of watercress, they make a delicious savoury snack.

Bon appétit!

Yours sincerely

David Hoult
Principal

61

148 Montpelier Rd,
Brighton,
East Sussex,
BN1 2LQ.

Laura Ashley,
Customer Services,
PO Box 19,
Newtown,
Powys,
SY16 1DZ

Dear Sir or Madam,

I have come up with something quite extraordinary, not to say revolutionary, and I want to share this idea with you for the betterment of mankind. I do not look for remuneration for my idea, just acknowledgement for my creative endeavor.

And what is my brilliant idea? Are you ready? Here it comes: round-buttock flies! It will probably take a few minutes to sink in, so just take a seat and ponder the possibilities.

Now people can pee and poo without undoing belts, etc. With one effortless unzipping they can relieve themselves in moments and be zipped up and back on the road in no time whatsoever. Of course, this will only be the case if, like me they choose not to wear undergarments. But even if they are prudish and still require the security of netherwear, there is another quite elegant solution: underpants that also have round-buttock flies! That covers all possibilities doesn't it?

I hope you have sufficiently recovered to now realize how important a breakthrough this is, and I expect you will want to get back to me on this as a matter of some urgency. I do look forward to your reply.

Yours truly,

Arthur Smithkins.

LAURA ASHLEY

Customer Services,
P.O. Box 19, Newtown, Powys SY16 1DZ
Tel. 0871 2302301 Fax. 01686 622183
e.mail : customer.services@lauraashley.com
website: www.lauraashley.com

Mr A Smithkins
148 Montpelier Road
Brighton
E Sussex
BN1 2LQ

Ref: 112779

29 July 2004

Dear Mr Smithkins,

Thank you for your letter received by us on 29 July 2004 .

We are writing to advise that this is being looked into as a matter of priority and we will contact you again in the very near future.

Please accept our apologies for any inconvenience caused in the meantime.

Yours sincerely,

Customer Services
LAURA ASHLEY

LAURA ASHLEY

Customer Services,
P.O. Box 19, Newtown, Powys SY16 1DZ
Tel. 0871 2302301 Fax. 01686 622183
e.mail : customer.services@lauraashley.com
website: www.lauraashley.com

Mr A Smithkins
148 Montpelier Road
Brighton
E Sussex
BN1 2LQ

Ref: 112779 /AFM

29 July 2004

Dear Mr Smithkins,

Thank you for your recent letter.

We do appreciate receiving comments from customers regarding the design of our clothing range, we find feedback useful and I would like to thank you for taking the time to write to us with your idea.

Whilst I recognize your enthusiasm, I am afraid that your idea is not a design feature that we would incorporate into any of our clothing in the foreseeable future.

Once again, I would like to thank you for writing to us.

Yours sincerely

Alison Murray
Customer Relations Manager
Customer Services
LAURA ASHLEY

148 Montpelier Rd,
Brighton,
East Sussex,
BN1 2LQ.

Blackpool Citizen's Advice Bureau,
6-10 Whitegate drive,
Devonshire Square,
Blackpool,
FY3 9AQ

Dear Sir or Madam,

I am writing to you because I am hoping you may be able to help me. In a month's time my nephew, Mally, will be coming to stay with me at my home in Brighton. He is coming to visit me, but he is also coming to take part in a 'Rocky Horror Picture Show' convention. I am 78 and I'm afraid to say that this 'Rocky Horror Picture Show' has passed me by, so to speak. I would, however, like to surprise my nephew and that is why I am writing to you.

Do you know anything about the 'Timewarp'? I am reliably informed that it is some sort of dance performed in your underwear. From what I can gather it is not an especially difficult dance, but it does involve a little pelvic thrusting, and possibly a jump to the left and/or right. Would it be possible for you to send me any information that you think relevant to my situation?

I can assure you that Mally will be a very surprised nephew indeed, if he is greeted by me in my front garden doing the 'Timewarp'!

I very much hope that you can be of some assistance to me.

Yours truly,

Molly Marsden (Retired).

Blackpool Citizens Advice Bureau

6-10 Whitegate Drive
Devonshire Square
Blackpool
FY3 9AQ

Advice Line   0870 1264090
Fax   01253 308420
www.blackpoolcab.org.uk e-mail: advice@blackpoolcab.org.uk

Manager   Marie Blackshaw

29th July, 2004

Ms Molly Marsden
148 Montpelier Road,
Brighton,
East Sussex.
BN1 2LQ

Dear Ms Marsden,

Thank you for your lovely letter, in which you asked if we could provide relevant information about the 'Timewarp'.

The best sources of information are currently available on the Internet and to assist you we have printed a small selection of information of relevance to your enquiry. Website addresses are printed at the bottom of each print out.

Item 1	Outlines the words to the Timewarp song. As you will see from this, it sets out the moves involved. You would certainly need to view the dance in action and in conjunction with the music to gain maximum benefit.
Item 2	Underwear is as you say, traditionally worn at the show. This usually consists of stockings, suspenders, corset and feather boa. This print out from the Official Rocky Horror Show Web Site offers some suggestions for outfits, including what not to wear. This site also provides an outline of the steps accompanying the music.
Item 3	Local Libraries in your area provide free internet facilities and a Video/DVD loans service. Why not borrow a copy of The Rocky Horror Picture Show on DVD or Video for viewing at home. This way you would be able to see the dance steps in action, together with the costumes worn by participants. The attached list, shows which libraries in your area have the Rocky Horror Picture Show in stock.

Alternatively, if you have the details of the Convention you could try contacting the organisers to see if they know of anyone who would be willing/able to demonstrate the dance moves for you!

*Community
Legal Service*

Registered Charity no 511537   General advice on any subject
Community Legal Service specialist level advice in Welfare Benefits and Debt

The show is famed for audience participation, why not enlist the help of some friends and neighbours to help you learn the moves.

Do let us know how you get on, I'm sure as you say, your nephew will be very surprised and no doubt entertained by your welcome.

Yours sincerely,

Marie Blackshaw

Marie Blackshaw
Manager

148 Montpelier Rd,
Brighton,
East Sussex,
BN1 2LQ.

Henkel Loctite Adhesives Ltd,
Watchmead,
Welwyn Garden City,
Herts,
AL7 1JB

Dear Sir or Madam,

I am writing to you in the hope that you may be able to help me. At present I work as an entertainer in and around the Brighton area. My stage name is 'Archie Arachnid' and, as the name suggests, I spend a lot of my time dressed up as a spider. People hire me for all sorts of events (weddings, barmitzvahs, hen night's etc) where I manifest myself as either a Black Widow or a Tarantula.

Oftentimes I am only required to crawl around the specified venue, ensnaring the odd, unsuspecting guest. However, on occasion I also like to perform in a static spider-like position. This is most effective when I can be 'cemented' to the ceiling of the proposed venue long before the guests are due to arrive. In the past this has lent my act a 'surprise' factor that the public usually find very entertaining.

To facilitate this I have been using a well-known glue in order to adhere myself to venue ceilings. This glue has proved to be satisfactory until recently. Unfortunately one or two 'accidents' of late have made me call into question the adhering qualities of the aforementioned glue. It's one thing being surprised by looking up and finding a six-foot Tarantula eyeing you from the ceiling above; it's quite another when the spider, through no fault of its own, drops on your head without warning (I weigh in at 17 Stone, and that's not counting the weight of the spider costume).

I am now desperately seeking a replacement adhesive to replace that which I have used up until now. Do you manufacture a glue that you think might suit my purposes? I need a glue which is relatively fast acting and which can easily bond hair to paint work. It goes without saying that I will need to buy any such glue in industrial-sized quantities. Do you provide discounts for bulk orders?

I do hope you can get back to me with the relevant information requested above, and with suggestions as to which products you would recommend.

Yours truly,

Gary Flowers.

Henkel

A Brand Like a Friend

Henkel Loctite Adhesives Ltd

5th August 2004

Mr G Flowers
148 Montpelier Road
Brighton
East Sussex
BN1 2LQ

Dear Gary (AKA Archie),

Thank you for your entertaining letter regarding your dilemma.

Much to my surprise when I opened your letter it drew me into a land of fantasy and fear. The arachnophobia I have suffered from for many years since my time up in the jungle and made my hands sweat along with beads of perspiration dripped over my brow. It's the little one that create this fear let alone a 17 stone monster. I hid behind a chair just watching Harry Potter and the Chamber of Secrets.

In answer to your question, the strength achieved in a bond is dependant on:

- The area.
- Materials (including surface finish).
- Loads applied.
- Conditions.

I guess you are going to bond the area of your hands in the gloves and knees. I estimate the total area is approximately $5760mm^2$ and 17 stone or 108kg being the load, therefore you need an adhesive that will exhibit sufficient load bearing capacity.

I guess your need to stick yourself immediately would not be realistic, as even a cyanoacrylate adhesive would take up to 12 hours to obtain the full strength. Health and safety regulations would not allow us to recommend a glue for these purposes, so it is with great regret (and some relief to my condition) that I must tell you we can not advise an application for your project, apart from you should not attempt this act !

Your sincerely
HENKEL LOCTITE ADHESIVES LIMITED

MIKE NORTH
TECHNOLOGY SPECIALIST

LOCTITE

Address:
Henkel Loctite AdhesivesLtd
Watchmead,
Welwyn Garden City
Herts. AL7 1JB UK
Phone: +44 (0)1707 358800
Fax: +44 (0)1707 358900
www.loctite.com

Registered No. 3819935
England
Registered Address:
Henkel Loctite Adhesives Ltd
Apollo Court
2 Bishop Square Business Park
Hatfield, Herts. AL10 9EY
www.henkel.com

69

148 Montpelier Rd,
Brighton,
East Sussex,
BN1 2LQ.

Mid Sussex Models,
13 Junction Rd,
Burgess Hill,
West Sussex,
RH15 0HR

Dear Sir or Madam,

I wonder if you can help me? At present I am urgently looking for a Naomi Campbell type model. Do you have anything like this in stock? I am not looking to buy such a model outright, but rather to hire the model for a long weekend. I would be more than happy to lay down a hefty deposit on such a model so you can be assured of its safe return.

If you don't have a Naomi Campbell type model, do you have anything resembling Kate Moss or Claudia Schiffer? I would much prefer Naomi Campbell, but I'd settle for either of the others if push came to shove!

Also, could you tell me if your models come with 'complete' outfits of clothing? I am hoping to go to Monte Carlo for the weekend and I would therefore like the models to come with appropriate outfits suitable for wining, dining and ballroom dancing. It would be prudent to have additional swimwear included in case the weather is clement down on the Riviera.

If you could write back to me with relevant costs I would be most grateful. Please do not hesitate to include any additional information that you think appropriate.

Yours truly,

Guy Piran.

PS. If the price is right, I may well consider hiring a number of models!

Mid Sussex Models

MODEL TRAINS, CARS, BOATS, RADIO CONTROL, DOLLS HOUSES, COLLECTIBLES, ETC.
13 Junction Road, Burgess Hill, West Sussex. RH15 0HR

midsussexmodels@btinternet.com   VAT No. 699 2714 77   Tel: 01444 232972
Fax: 01444 239723

29/07/04

Dear Guy Piran,

Thankyou for your enquiry re Naomi Campbell type models. We are very sorry to say we are unable to help you with the items you require.

We do hope you have success in finding these models, and you will have a good trip to Monte Carlo.

Best wishes.

Yours sincerely,

Roger

ROGER LUNN
Proprietor

71

148 Montpelier Rd,
Brighton,
East Sussex,
BN1 2LQ.

Peperami,
Unilever Bestfoods UK,
Brooke House,
Crawley,
West Sussex,
RH10 9RQ

Dear Peperami,

You're a bit of an animal – that's for sure! My partner and I are animals too, and we simply love your product. You've got lots of imitators out there but we can assure you that none of your competitors reach the spot quite like you do. And what's more none of your competitors come with a 'protective' sheath – that's why Peperami's the only one for us.

However, do you think it at all possible that you could bring out a Peperami just a little bit longer than the present product? Dare I suggest one that's twice as long? This would undoubtedly double the pleasure that we get from your product.

We've tried taping a couple together but it just never seems to work. After a couple of hours or so the structural integrity is always severely challenged. In addition to this, we've occasionally had 'accidents' which have left one or both of us severely compromised, as it were.

I'm sure you're the type of company that takes a keen interest in what your customers think, and that's why both Derick and I know you'll give our request due consideration.

Yours truly,

Guy Piran.

Ref: 367311
Date: 30 July 2004

Peperami Consumer Care
Freepost NATE139
Milton Keynes
MK9 1BR

Freephone: 0800 242422

G Piran   367311
148 Montpelier Road
Brighton
East Sussex
BN1 2LQ

Dear Sir/Madam

Thank you for your recent letter regarding the size and length of our Peperami.

We were so pleased to learn that you and your partner have managed to receive so much pleasure from the use of our product, and hope that this will continue to be the case for many years to come.

Whilst it is always pleasing to hear such positive comments from our consumers, we are concerned to learn that you are not always fully satisfied by one Peperami at a time. We have notified the Brand Management that you have requested a double length portion, and they will be in a position to give this due consideration for future developments.

We were also concerned to learn that you have been using tape to enhance your Peperami pleasure, and that this has led to you both being left in a position of compromise. Please be assured that our product was fully tested before its launch to ensure that it would retain the correct rigidity, right down to that last inch.

Thank you again for your feedback. I hope that both Derick and yourself will continue to enjoy Peperami, and will accept the enclosed vouchers as a gesture of goodwill.

Yours faithfully

Gerard Walters
Consumer Care Advisor

--
Enclosures:
2 x Unilever Bestfoods Coupon £1

148 Montpelier Rd,
Brighton,
East Sussex,
United Kingdom,
BN1 2LQ.

Loren Leman,
Office of the Lieutenant Governor,
550W7th Avenue,
Suite 1700,
Anchorage,
AK 99501,
USA.

Dear Loren,

I am writing to you as chairman of the Burnt Alaska Diaspora. Comprising both professional and amateur chefs from all over the United Kingdom, our organisation now boasts some 200 members. What we all share in common is a keen regard for verisimilitude and authentic literalness when it comes to interpreting various culinary dishes. In simple terms, it means we follow recipes to the letter.

We are hoping to organise a visit to Alaska for some of our members in December of this year. We will be basing ourselves in Anchorage, and hope to stay for between 10-14 days.

While we are there we would dearly like to live up to our society name and burn a little bit of Alaska. Could you suggest the right people to contact in order to facilitate our wishes? We don't envisage spending any more than a couple of afternoons doing any burning. The rest of the time we'll be doing what other tourists do.

When we do burn, we will be doing it together, as it were. We consider that this will cause the least inconvenience to local landowners and/or wildlife. We will also not be using any combustion agent that could cause burning to get out of hand (gasoline, dynamite, etc).

Presumably there are some places near to Anchorage that are not heavily populated and where a little bit of burning will not cause any long-term damage. Would it be possible for you to provide a list of any such areas, along with a price guide as to how much we might have to pay per metre squared.

I bet you don't get requests like this every day, but we are quite an unusual diaspora, to say the least.

I very much look forward to hearing from you in due course.

Yours truly,

David Carafe.

74

Lieutenant Governor Loren Leman

October 22, 2004

Mr. David Carafe
148 Montpelier Rd
East Sussex, United Kingdom
BN1 2LQ

Dear Mr. Carafe,

I am pleased to welcome your organization to Alaska. I'm certain that you will enjoy our beautiful State and find that we have wonderful accommodations.

In your letter you inquired about designated areas in which you could ignite fires in the Anchorage area. Here are the addresses for the appropriate people for you to communicate with regarding your request:

Municipality of Anchorage
Anchorage Fire Department
122 E. 4th. Avenue
Anchorage, AK 99501
907-267-4936

Department of Natural Resources
Division of Forestry
Joe Stam – Fire Program Manager
550 W 7th Ave Ste 1450
Anchorage, AK 99501
907-269-8467

Although you may find the weather in Alaska chilly in December, you will find our people warm and helpful. Enjoy your visit and your burn!

Sincerely,

Loren Leman
Lieutenant Governor

148 Montpelier Rd,
Brighton,
East Sussex,
BN1 2LQ.

National Coal Mining Museum,
Caphouse Colliery,
Wakefield

Dear Sir or Madam,

I am writing to you as chairman of the Brighton Underground Theatre Society, based here in Sussex. As part of our forthcoming schedule of events we are hoping to put on a production of Orpheus in the Underworld towards the end of the year. To this end we are actively seeking out suitable dramatic venues in which to perform this theatrical piece.

We are hoping that it may be possible for us to make use of one of your abandoned mineshafts for our production. We desperately want our production to feel authentic and we therefore won't need you to provide anything expensive like electricity. Instead we will be bringing our own safety torches that can burn for anything up to twelve hours. We also envisage making use of ropes and pulleys to get the audience down into the Orphean underworld, which means you won't have to service anything mechanical.

We would have to be on site the day before the performance in order to make all the preparations. Our production, for example, makes use of nearly 75 specially trained dwarves who appear during the performance as evil demons. These dwarves need to be in place long before the audience arrives.

We also need to make use of a small chamber orchestra who must remain hidden from the audience. We want the music to drift hauntingly into the makeshift auditorium as if it was part of a film soundtrack by Tarkovsky.

Also, could you advise us as to the health and safety issues of using small firecrackers? Towards the end of the production we need to give the impression that the theatrical underworld is breaking down, and we feel that actual firecrackers are intrinsic in giving this impression to the audience.

We would be hoping to rent the mine for the duration of our production. This we can do at a flat rate if you so wish, or we could come to an agreement based on sharing the ticket sales royalties. Perhaps when you write back you could address which of these two options you would prefer. If there are any other questions that you may have then please feel free to include them in any future correspondence.

I very much look forward to hearing back from you soon.

Yours truly,

Guy Alexander Piran Mole.

NATIONAL COAL MINING MUSEUM

for England

Mr G A P Mole
148 Montpelier Rd
Brighton
E Sussex
BN1 2LQ

06/08/04

Ref: RS/BUTS/01

Dear Mr Mole

Re: Orpheus in the Underworld

Thank you for letter (undated) relating to the above performance. Whilst it sounds like an interesting project your letter throws up several questions:

How large an area would be required for the auditorium?
How many would you anticipate the audience numbering?
How long is the production (it is quite cold down the mine)?

Other practical issues would revolve around getting the audience to the auditorium, our cage takes 19 people at once and an up and down cycle takes 12 minutes. To get the dwarves down would take an hour in itself. It would not be possible to use firecrackers in the mine on the grounds of Health and Safety.

Before determining which payment scheme is preferable it would be sensible to overcome some of the issues raised. If you wish to discuss this venture further please contact me at the Museum.

Yours sincerely

Richard Saward

Richard Saward
Commercial Director

National Coal Mining Museum for England

Caphouse Colliery, New Road, Overton, Wakefield, West Yorkshire, WF4 4RH
Tel: (01924) 848806   Fax: (01924) 840694   email: info@ncm.org.uk   website: www.ncm.org.uk

Chairman : the Rt. Hon. the Baroness Lockwood   **Director** : Dr. M. L. Faull   **Secretary** : Dr. M. L. Faull.
REGISTERED IN ENGLAND AS A LIMITED COMPANY BY GUARANTEE NO. 1702426. VAT REG. NO. 457 5483 14
REG. CHARITY : 517325. REGISTERED OFFICE: CAPHOUSE COLLIERY

148 Montpelier Rd,
Brighton,
East Sussex,
BN1 2LQ.

Louis Hughes Sperm Donation Centre,
99 Harley Street,
London,
W1G 6AP

Dear Sir or Madam,

My name is Arthur Wesley Smitherington and I live here in Brighton, Sussex. For some time now I have been involved in a 'professional' project, which has meant that I have had to masturbate on a regular basis. I now have nearly two gallons of semen on the go. All my sperm are stored in a yoghurt-making machine, which keeps them at a regular temperature of 38.3 degrees.

I have recently considered offering my sperm on the Internet for free, but I have now gone off the idea.

Would you like to have my sperm? I could offer it to you at a special discount, as it were.

Perhaps you would care to contact me at the above address if you need any further information.

Yours truly,

A.W. Smitherington.

DR LOUIS HUGHES
99 HARLEY STREET
LONDON W1G 6AQ
TELEPHONE 020 7935 9004
FACSIMILE 020 7935 6494

5 August, 2004

A.W. Smitherington
148 Montpelier Road
Brighton
East Sussex
BN1 2LQ

Dear Mr Smitherington

In response to your recent letter concerning a 'professional project' you have been involved in. Unfortunately we are not interested in your commodity, as we have no immediate plans for any wallpapering on site.

If your volume is accurate this must have taken you considerable time i.e. in excess of a year so perhaps the Guinness Book of Records would be interested in one of the most useless collections, let alone how many standard yoghurt makers you have used.

For the record if you have been keeping your sperm at 38.3° then it must be well fermented by now. As it is well documented that i) sperm need to be stored at a lower body temperature to normal (which is actually 37°) and ii) once produced they start to die off, irrespective of the temperature stored at.

Yours sincerely

L. Sheahan

148 Montpelier Rd,
Brighton,
East Sussex,
BN1 2LQ.

Ullswater Tourist Information,
Glenridding,
Penrith,
Cumbria,
CA11 0PA

Dear Sir or Madam,

Hi, my name is Laura Gurie and I come from Boulder, Colorado, in the United States of America. I have just arrived in the United Kingdom, and at present I am staying in the quaint coastal resort of Brighton on the south coast. I will be here for a week while I explore London and the Southeast. I am very excited to be here in England as this is my first time here.

Once I have finished doing London I will have a couple of days left over to do another bit of England. The Lake District is a place that has been personally recommended to me as an area well worth doing, and that's why I'm writing to you.

Say, for example, I only have one day, how much of the Lake District do you think I could fit in? Would it be possible to do the whole thing even?

I have been told that you can take the monorail round the twelve highest peaks, and I would definitely like to book this in advance. Will this take more than a couple of hours?

I am also very keen to take a cruise on Lake Windermere in order to try and catch a glimpse of the Windermere Monster. I have been told, though I find it hard to believe, that 'Mabel' is a 10,000 Ib Trout. Is this true? If it is true then how old is she?

If I have time then I would also like to take in the Leprechaun Circus, although I am not sure where this is located.

I very much look forward to hearing from you soon, as I'd like to make all the necessary arrangements.

Yours truly,

Laura Gurie.

Laura Gurie
148 Montpelier Rd
Brighton
East Sussex
BN1 2LG

29 July 2004

Dear Laura

Your letter has made us smile.
We think that someone has been having fun with you.

The Lake District is a large area containing 13 lakes each surrounded by mountains. It is 40 miles from one end to the other.
It will take you 8 hours from Brighton, maybe longer by train or bus.
One day would only allow you to see a very small area.
We do not have a monorail. It would take a feat of wonder meant to design one in this Park.
There is a 'fictional' Loch Ness monster in Scotland. This is another 4 hours from the borders of England.
Some say that if you visit the Isle Of Man that you can talk to the little people at the bridge near Peel
The real Leprechauns live in Ireland. We would love to know if they have formed a circus.

Best Wishes

Bowness Bay Staff

Lake District
National Park Authority
Lake District National Park Authority
Bowness Bay TIC
Glebe Road
Bowness-on-Windermere
Cumbria
LA23 3HJ
Tel: 015394 42895
Fax: 015394 88005

Why not visit us for further information and ideas . . .
we look forward to seeing you

Email: Bownesstic@lake-district.gov.uk
Website: www.lake-district.gov.uk

A member of the Association
of National Park Authorities

A member of the Federation of Nature
and National Parks of Europe

...*with compliments*

**We are here to look after the National Park, helping people to enjoy its
beauty, whilst fostering the well-being of those who live and work here.**

Timothy Walker,
Chief Executive and Artistic Director,
London Philharmonic Orchestra,
89 Albert Embankment,
London,
SE1 7TP

Dear Timothy,

I am writing to you to offer my services as a conductor. I don't know if you have any openings at the moment, but the minute one does come up I would like you to give my application serious consideration.

I have been a pianist all my life (grade 5) and I am also something of a guitarist (rhythm). The fact that I can also play the penny whistle means that I am a bit of a multi-instrumentalist. I think this will be very useful in my conducting, and I know that there are some conductors out there who can barely play one instrument! How they expect to empathise fully with an orchestra I will never know.

I have been conducting since the beginning of last year and I am completely self-taught. I started out in quite a small way with a drumstick and Mozart. I would put Mozart on the CD on a repeat setting and stand there for literally hours waving my drumstick in the air. I laugh now at my simple unashamed enthusiasm.

At the moment there isn't a composer, alive or dead, that I can't do; and what is more I now have a complete collection of conducting batons (I keep the drumstick on the wall to remind me of my humble beginnings). I have learned from some of the great living conductors. I have co-conducted every televised BBC Proms concert for 2002 and 2003. While the well-known conductor is doing his stuff in front of a live audience, I am doing my stuff in front of the television. I assure you I know all the moves – large ones, small ones, and those kind of flowing ones in between. I am now also very good at moving my head whilst rolling my eyes. When you're doing big movements with the baton and rolling your eyes at the same time it's really something else. Would it sound crazy to say that I feel a little divine? I guess all conductors are a little crazy so I'm no different from the rest. Having said that, I do go to the barbers once a week to keep my hair in trim. I think it is very important to be neat and tidy if you expect an orchestra to have any respect for you, that's why I don't understand why so many of these so-called modern 'conductors' get away with their unkempt condition.

If it is the case that you do have a conductor at the moment might I suggest that you consider how much you could save by having me instead. I'll be happy to start off on half of what you pay at present for conducting services. I can't say fairer than that, now can I?

I should be most grateful if you could get back to me on this as soon as possible. Your orchestra is definitely my first choice but if I do not hear back from you I will put out multiple applications to other orchestras, some of them foreign. I think it would be an awful pity if natural homegrown talent like myself were to be lured away by the Russian Rouble or the Yankee Dollar.

If you feel you need to see me in person then just drop me a line and we'll arrange a date and time – I'll obviously bring all my batons for you to have a close look.

I very much look forward to hearing from you.

Yours truly,

Gary Huggins.

London **Philharmonic** Orchestra

Mr Gary Huggins
148 Montpelier Rd
East Sussex
BN1 2LQ

20 August 2004

Dear Mr Huggins

I very much enjoyed reading your letter concerning conducting opportunities with the London Philharmonic Orchestra.

Would you mind if I shared it with others through the Orchestra's quarterly newsletter?

Kindest regards

Timothy Walker AM
Chief Executive and Artistic Director

148 Montpelier Rd,
Brighton,
BN1 2LQ

03.09.04

Timothy Walker,
Chief Executive & Artistic Director,
London Philharmonic Orchestra,
89 Albert Embankment,
London,
SE1 7TP

Dear Timothy,

Thank you so much for responding to my earnest supplication. I knew that of all the orchestras in the world the London Philharmonic would give my application due and proper consideration.

And let me say right now that I would be most honoured if you were to consider my initial correspondence worthy to be printed in your orchestra's quarterly newsletter. I'm a considerably better conductor than I am a writer (CSE grade iii would you believe), but I'm entirely excited that you've found some merit in my remedial lexicography.

You will be pleased to know that I have co-conducted the entire series of Proms 2004, and what is more I am now advertising to take on conducting students for the first time. I envisage that within months I could have a whole host of new conducting talent. I shall provide expert tuition and guidance for free, but they will have to buy their own batons. A conductor's batons are sacrosanct are they not?

I hope you would consider one further small request. If you are to publish my humble letter in your quarterly newsletter, could I ask that you send me 4 or 5 copies of the newsletter itself? That way I can give away a copy or two to family and friends. My mother will be over the moon, I can tell you!

Thank you once again.

Yours truly,

Gary Huggins.

148 Montpelier Rd,
Brighton,
East Sussex,
BN1 2LQ.

Vidal Sasson,
130 Sloane Street,
London.

Dear Sir or Madam,

My name is Alice Fellatio and I play bass guitar in the punk band 'Dogbreath'. On a number of occasions in the past I have visited one of your salons for your talented staff to sort out my unruly hair. I haven't been for the last couple of years because for the last amount of time I've had a Mohican. Mohicans do take a bit of maintenance but it's all stuff you can do at home for yourself. I did, however have the original Mohican done in one of your salons, and I expect that's why it's grown out as well as it has.

Would it be possible for you to do the same for my pet dog 'Star Wars'? He is a Longhaired Yak Poodle, which is a breed that originated in central Asia. He stands roughly three foot tall at his haunches and is as soft as butter. The grooming clinic that I take him to refused to have a go (I don't think they like punks!!), but I always wanted him to have a professional cut anyway.

If needs be, I could bring him in for a consultation first in order for you to have a good look. It would be quite a job undoubtedly, but he's going to be our band's mascot and the record company are therefore happy to pay for his doggy Mohican.

I really hope you can help 'Star Wars' and me.

Yours truly,

A. Fellatio.

VIDAL SASSOON
130 SLOANE STREET
LONDON
SW1X 9AT
Tel: 020 7730 7288

148 Montpelier Road
Brighton
East Sussex
BN1 2LQ

30/07/2004

Dear A Fellatio

Thank you for your recent letter. Fellicitations. I must admit your letter has been a bone of contention here with some people feeling they would be in the doghouse if I asked them to cut "Star Wars" hair, as we only cut bipeds.

If you would like to discuss it further I suggest you contact our Creative Director, Willi. However, we would love you to come back to our salons as a client to sort out your unruly hair again, but could only admire your Yak from a distance.

I must say we haven't heard "Dogbreath's" music although I see on the internet there is Dogbreath Records. Is the music very turgid?

Sorry we can't be of more help

Yours sincerely

A Condom
Manager

148 Montpelier Rd,
Brighton,
East Sussex,
BN1 2LQ.

Andrew Lloyd Webber,
The Really Useful Group,
22 Tower Street,
London,
WC2H 9TW

Dear Andrew,

I can't tell you how excited I am! I have been labouring for years to come up with a brilliant and original idea for a musical, and now I have it. And forgive me if I say this, but it's pure genius. You know how you based Cats on a famous poem? Well, this Musical is based on a poem too! Only this time I wrote the poem in the first instance, and now I've come up with the idea for the musical. It's called 'Ducks', and just as Cats was all to do with cats, 'Ducks' is all to do with ducks.

Imagine this, a stage where the middle has been turned into a large and realistic-looking pond. The stage lighting makes it look like early morning and you can hear the sound of birds tweetering in the realistic-looking trees. Suddenly one solitary duck head appears up out of the water, looks from left to right and then directly out to the audience. What the audience can't possibly know as yet, because they can only see the head, is that this is Delilah Duck, and after a suitable dramatic pause she starts to sing. I'm still working on this opening number, but I'll give you the beginning so that you get the feel:

Quack, quack, quack, quack, quack
I'm just little old Delilah Duck
Quack, quack, quack, quack, quack
I roll around in the country muck Quacketty, quacketty, quacketty, quack.

Quack, quack, quack, quack, quack
My brothers and sisters and me
Quack, quack, quack, quack, quack
Know what it means to be free
Quacketty, quacketty, quacketty, quack. . .

There's probably going to be at least three or four more verses to this number to really draw the audience into the world of the ducks. Incidentally, when Delilah Duck mentions 'brothers and sisters' in the second verse, that's when twelve other duck heads appear in unison in the pond. That makes a total of thirteen. And Delilah is the unlucky thirteenth duck (we find out why much later in the musical when the pond has been visited by the evil Farmer Giles).

Overall I can see people flocking to this musical, especially children. Actually a good many children are scared of cats, you know, but I can't think of one child who's scared of ducks. That's why I think this is a sure-fire winner. We could even have a little bit of audience participation when it came down to some of the 'quacking' - everybody knows how to quack like a duck, and there's quacking in most of the songs to really bring it home to the viewing public that these are not just actors and actresses on stage but in fact real ducks.

I feel sure that you will definitely be interested in this, and I can make plans to come up to London to see you at very short notice. At the moment I work in a kitchen but I don't want to do this any more. And anyway, now that I've come up with a top West End show I won't have to look back at my past anymore - and that's a blessing.

I look forward to hearing from you very soon, and I am very, very excited!!

Yours truly,

Gary Flowers.

THE REALLY USEFUL GROUP LIMITED
22 Tower Street, London WC2H 9TW
Tel: 020 7240 0880 Fax: 020 7240 1204 www.reallyuseful.com

From the office of Andrew Lloyd Webber

29th July 2004

Gary Flowers
148 Montpelier Road
Brighton
East Sussex
BN1 2LQ

Dear Gary

Thank you for your recent letter to Lord Lloyd-Webber. I am responding on his behalf.

I am afraid that Andrew has not seen your letter. As I'm sure you will understand, he receives a great many proposals from all over the world and it is simply impossible for him to consider any unsolicited material in the first instance.

Unfortunately therefore, Andrew will not be able to help you with your idea for a musical. His production schedule is also so hectic that he is unable to take on any additional commitments for the foreseeable future.

I am sorry to send a disappointing reply and wish you every success with your idea, which incidentally reminds me of the recent musical about ducks and the ugly duckling called "Honk"!.........

With kind regards

Yours sincerely

Kate Losowsky
Assistant PA to Andrew Lloyd Webber

148 Montpelier Rd,
Brighton,
East Sussex,
BN1 2LQ.

Butcher's Choice,
Butcher's Petcare Ltd,
Crick,
Northampton,
NN6 7TZ

Dear Sir or Madam,

I am writing to you with a specific question relating to your product. Is it safe for human beings to eat Butcher's Choice? I remember once being told that all dog food had to come up to the standards that one would expect for human food. If this is the case then your dog food, above all others, should be one of the safest.

The reason that I have to ask this is because I have got into a bit of a predicament with regards my family. I am married with four children. My family have always been supportive of me in all manner of ways, but not when it comes down to my cooking. All my children and my husband, Philip, would much rather eat pre-prepared food than anything which I had anything to do with preparing. This has led to arguments and at times extreme disappointment and frustration for me.

It was, then, with some relish that on my birthday I forced my family to remain at home and not go out to a restaurant as is customary . I knew that on that particular day there would be no arguments to do with my cooking and at the last minute, instead of adding two pounds of minced steak to my Bolognaise I added 2 large cans of Beef Butcher's Choice.

I know this sounds insane, but I wanted to teach them all a lesson that they would never forget. I was going to let them dutifully eat up their food and then show them the empty cans as proof of what they'd just eaten.

Imagine my surprise, then, when Jemima, my youngest daughter finished her portion of Butcher's Choice 'Bolognaise', and actually asked me for seconds. I nearly fell off my chair. Of all my family she is the most anti-mummy's cooking! I gave her seconds and replenished the plates of the rest of my family. When that main course was complete there wasn't a scrap of 'bolognaise' left in the pan or on anyone's plates. I carefully carried the plates into the kitchen and furtively got rid of the two empty cans of Butcher's Choice.

I have to tell you that since that eventful day my family and I have dined on your product whether it be in curries, chilli-con-carne's, or even stroganoffs. I have remained undiscovered because I always wait till I am alone in the house to 'decant' your tinned product into conveniently sized Tupperware. This I store in the fridge until I need to use it. I even keep a little in the freezer as back up.

I have to tell you that this secret use of your product has created a much happier family environment for me, and I am at last appreciated for something which I had almost given up on.

I am hoping that you can write back to me confirming that Butcher's Choice does come up to human safety standards, especially when it's cooked. If it's safe straight from the can then I'll be able to make pate's, etc.

I should be most grateful if you can get back to me on this as soon as possible.

Yours truly,

Anne Wayward.

5 August 2004

Mrs Wayward
148 Montpelier Road
Brighton
East Sussex
BN1 2LQ

Dear Mrs Wayward

Thank you for your letter regarding Butcher's Choice.

We were surprised at your use of this product as Butcher's Choice is a quality food designed specifically for small dogs.

Whilst the name for this range in mainland Europe is "Gastronomia", I can assure you Gordon Ramsey has never requested the recipe from us for use in his kitchens!

We are confident the contents would not harm a human as all the ingredients are fit for human use and have passed strict food guidelines.

The Bolognaise story is amusing however your suggestion using Choice as a pate does seem more fitting – revenge being a dish best served cold......

However, we cannot bring ourselves to recommend you continue to use it in your cooking, no matter how shiny and healthy your family's hair, skin and teeth have become....

I hope you are able to find alternative recipes your family will enjoy. Alternatively, may I suggest you buy them their own cookbooks for Christmas and encourage them to spend some quality time in the kitchen?

Bon appétit!

Hazel Major (Mrs)
Consumer & Customer Services Manager

Consumer Servic
Butcher's Pet Care
Crick
Northamptonshire
NN6 7TZ

The Rialto,
PO Box 309,
Norwich,
NR11 6LN

148 Montpelier Rd,
Brighton,
East Sussex,
BN1 2LQ.

Dear Poets,

I am writing to you to offer you a poem that I'm sure you will have to consider quite unique. I did not actually write this poem, but I feel I helped to inspire it. The poem itself can be said to come directly from the oral tradition – I have only acted as a recorder.

What makes this poem even more extraordinary is that in many ways it predates the human (homo sapien) era, even though it was only 'spoken' but a few weeks ago!

To avoid any further confusion I have to inform you that none other than my pet baboon, Shakespeare, composed this poem. Shakespeare and I have been working together for quite some time now. I started out reading children's stories and poetry to Shakespeare, which he thoroughly enjoyed. After some time I moved on to more serious and erudite material (Larkin, Proust, Schopenhauer…), and Shakespeare and I have never looked back.

The title of Shakespeare's poem is 'Ooh', and I present it to you here in full.

Ooh

Ohh-ooh-a-ooh-ooh,
Ohh-ooh-a-ooh-ohh,
Ooh-ooh;

Ooh-ooh-a-ooh-ooh,
Ooh-ooh-a-ooh-ooh,
Ooh-ooh.

Ooh-ooh-ooh-ooh-a-ooh;
Ooh-a-ooh.

I think that you will agree with me that this is quite stunning work for an ape, and worthy of being published alongside work produced by his more cerebral Homo Sapien cousins. You don't need me to tell you how much poetic rubbish there is out there and, conversely, how little good *baboon* poetry there is.

I very much look forward to hearing from you soon.

Yours truly,

Mark Maddon & Shakespeare.

THE RIALTO

**PO Box No 309 Aylsham
Norwich NR11 6LN England**

www.therialto.co.uk
Editor: Michael Mackmin

Dear Mark

Thank you for your
letter etc. — which I
enclose in case you haven't
a copy of the work in
question. On the whole
I prefer to publish the
poetic rubbish that I
get sent by people rather

ARTS COUNCIL
ENGLAND

Then this stuff by
your companion, but
thanks for thinking of
the magazine.

Best wishes
David Keen

United Kingdom Dangerous Sports Club

La Chute, 148 Montpelier Road, Brighton, East Sussex, BN1 2LQ.

Argyll & Bute Council,
Kilmory,
Lochgilphead,
PA31 8RT

Dear Sir or Madam,

I am writing to you as the acting chairman of the United Kingdom Dangerous Sports Club. A number of suggestions have been put forward for our 2005 schedule, and it looks like it's going to be a year to surpass all others. One of our most exciting suggestions has been put forward by our vice-president, Saul Davies, and it is with this in mind that I am writing to you now.

Saul has connections with a Japanese touring circus company that will be putting on shows throughout Scotland next summer. Part of this extraordinary troupe is an act involving a number of Kimodo dragons. This act is fairly similar to more traditional circus events involving lions or tigers. What Saul has suggested, and the Japanese circus agreed to in principle, is to borrow a number of the Kimodo Dragons for a weekend when they are not being used in circus performances. Making use of their specifically tailored transport we would then have the dragons ferried across to Mull.

We would like to make use of an area of land off the beaten track, as it were, and where there is a limited amount of indigenous animals and livestock. The dragons would then be released and, after a sufficient time interval, a number of our more intrepid sports club members would then embark in hot pursuit. Individually and in pairs they would then capture the beasts and ferry them back to the appointed rendezvous stations.

All of the dragons would wear harnesses with satellite tracking devices, so that any un-captured dragon could easily be tracked and recaptured after the event. This should qualm any fears that you may have that one of these animals might get clean away.

We would, of course, be more than willing to pay an appropriate fee for the use of the land, and, of course, make reparations to any farmer's livestock that accidentally gets in the way.

If you could write back to me as to your willingness to host this extraordinary and exciting event I would be most grateful. Please do not hesitate to include any further questions that you might have.

Yours truly,

Jasper Fjord.

Argyll and Bute Council
Comhairle Earra Ghàidheal agus Bhòid

Corporate Services
Director: Nigel Stewart

Our Ref: AST/DJM/3515

Legal and Protective Services

Your Ref:

Kilmory, Lochgilphead PA31 8RT
Tel: 01546 - 604132 Fax: 01546 - 604373
DX No: 599700 LOCHGILPHEAD
24 August 2004
e-mail : sandy.taylor@argyll-bute.gov.uk
Website: www.argyll-bute.gov.uk

Jasper Fjord Esq
United Kingdom Dangerous Sports Club
La Chute
148 Montpelier Road
Brighton
East Sussex
BN1 2LQ

Dear Mr Fjord

ENQUIRY REGARDING KIMODO DRAGON RELEASE/CAPTURE EVENT

I refer to your recent communication in which you enquired about the possibility of hosting an event on the Island of Mull which would see the release, pursuit and subsequent capture of Kimodo dragons by members of your club.

In brief I must say that the Council would not support such an event for the following reasons:

a) the release of non-indigenous species into the wild requires a licence issued under the provisions of the Wildlife and Countryside Act 1981 issued by Scottish Natural Heritage. Having contacted the local office of Scottish Natural Heritage I can advise that that would not be granted.

b) the Council could not condone the deliberate release of dangerous animals with the foreseeable consequence(s) of injury to local wildlife and worse still the potential for harm to humans. This notwithstanding your compensation.

c) on the event of any such attack, it would undoubtedly constitute "unnecessary suffering" as described in the Protection of Animals Act 1912 (as amended).

d) the Council is pre-disposed against the use of animals for public performance and/or entertainment although not hitherto considered in that context, the Council be unlikely to consider the use of (dangerous) wild animals, as envisaged, any more favourably.

I repeat therefore that the Council would not welcome your proposal. Beyond that, both the Police and the Council's Animal Health and Welfare Officers would look closely at any such activity with a view to the investigation of formal enforcement proceed in respect of any statutory breach(es) in the event that such an activity was organised.

Yours sincerely

A S TAYLOR
Chief Protective Services Officer

If phoning please ask for: Sandy Taylor

Goldsmiths College of Art,
University of London,
New Cross,
London,
SE14 6NW

148 Montpelier Rd,
Brighton,
East Sussex,
BN1 2LQ.

Dear Sir or Madam,

I am writing to you to offer you my hand. I know that this will appear to be a most peculiar bequest, but this is a sincere offer and one which I have put a good deal of thought into.

I lost my hand some months ago in an accident with a chainsaw. The stump was in such a state once severed that it was impossible for the surgeons to even attempt to rejoin it to its rightful place on the end of my arm.

The loss of the hand has been an extreme tragedy for me because I have made my living up until recently playing flamenco guitar with the 'Alhambra Brothers'. The other members of the band have been extraordinarily kind and have even offered to help me to use my stump in some sort of rhythm capacity. I have declined their kind offers because I know that this would not be in keeping with the virtuoso musicianship that the' Alhambra Brothers' are famous for.

I have the hand stored inside a sealed plastic container deposited in my deep freeze. As you will no doubt have gathered from the above, it is the epitome of what a flamenco hand should be. It has long shapely fingers with thick long nails at the end of each of the fingers, including the thumb. It has very few hairs on it (I have never been a hirsute man!) and there is still good muscle definition.

In short I think it would be a good hand to be used in life-drawing classes, and that is why I am making this offer to you in the first instance.

On a number of occasions I have defrosted the hand for the benefit of neighbours, family and friends. I have never left it defrosted for more than an hour or so, before popping it back in the freezer again, and there has been very little degeneration. With the optimum care I would think that you could get a good deal of use out of it, perhaps even for a year or two.

If you were to be amenable to accepting my hand, then I should make the gift to you and then relinquish all rights to it in writing. The only thing that I would like to ask is that I be invited to the first life-drawing session to introduce my own hand to the students and staff, and then to watch the life-drawing session taking place. I should then quietly bid adieu to my ex-appendage and leave to get on with the rest of my life.

I really think that this will bring a certain amount of closure to what has been a very traumatic time for my family and I, and I hope you will carefully consider my bequest in the spirit with which it has been offered.

Yours truly,

Edward Coupe.

Goldsmiths
UNIVERSITY
OF LONDON

2 August 2004

DEPARTMENT OF VISUAL ARTS
Telephone   020 7919 7671
Fax   020 7919 7673
Email   j.jefferies@gold.ac.uk

Head of Department
Professor Janis Jefferies

Edward Coupe
148 Montpelier Road
Brighton
East Sussex
BN1 2LQ

Dear Mr Coupe

Thank you for your letter. We were extremely sorry to hear about your tragic accident.

Thank you for offering your hand to us. I am afraid that anatomy is not a subject on any of the Visual Arts Department programmes. I would suggest, however, that you write to:

> Ms Louise Evans
> London Anatomy Office
> Imperial College School of Medicine
> Charing Cross Hospital
> Fulham Palace Road
> London
> W6 8RF

Some medical faculties at London University offer anatomy drawing to small groups of students, and the London Anatomy Office would be a starting point for you.

Thanking you again and with all good wishes for the future.

Yours sincerely

Madeleine Dobson

Madeleine Dobson
Secretary
Visual Arts Office

Goldsmiths College, University of London, New Cross, London SE14 6NW
Main Telephone Number: 020 7919 7171   Web site: *www.goldsmiths.ac.uk*

GOLDSMITHS AIMS TO BE PRE-EMINENT IN THE STUDY AND PRACTICE OF CREATIVE, COGNITIVE, CULTURAL AND SOCIAL PROCESSES

Forest Enterprise Office,
Sherwood Forest District,
Edwinstowe,
Mansfield,
Notts,
NG21 9JL

148 Montpelier Rd,
Brighton,
East Sussex,
BN1 2LQ.

Dear Sir or Madam,

I am writing to you from Brighton, where I am a member of the Regress Society. There are now nearly 200 of us, and we feel we are now nearing the time that we would like to move en-masse to a place where we can live together full-time, as it were.

The regress society was founded in 1994 as a counterbalance to what many of us saw, and still see, as the imbalance and injustice of supposed 'progress' . On a philosophical level many of us believe that there needn't be an inevitability about 'progress' whatsoever, certainly not if a number of us join forces to actively dismantle any such 'progress' in a regressive manner.

Our society has now, amongst many other things, happily de-discovered the wheel, de-discovered fire, even de-discovered the existence of God. When we finally find ourselves in a suitable abode we are then aiming to de-discover language entirely too!

To this end, would you happen to know of any reasonably large area of Sherwood Forest where the Regress Society could happily go about de-discovering all manner of other things on our collective journey back to the primeval and beyond. We obviously need to be based somewhere a long way from any present day habitation, and also a good deal away from any lines of modern communication (roads, railways, etc).

Many of us have regressed from quite prominent jobs in the community, and we therefore have a quite sizeable amount of money pooled in order for us to purchase any virgin forest. Once we have purchased the aforementioned forest we would, of course, be leaving all other money, belongings, clothes, etc, in the outside 'progressive' world. Once in our new-found home we want to grunt, scavenge and swing from the trees proud and free.

I expect you don't get letters like this every day of the week, but I would hope that you can give our request careful consideration. We really don't envisage that we will have any untoward impact upon your native fauna and flora whatsoever, and once we're in there you hopefully won't see or hear from us ever again.

A similar application has been tended to the Congolese government in Africa, but our society would far prefer to base ourselves in Sherwood Forest. We feel that in Africa, where deforestation is occurring on an accelerated basis, even if we found a remote spot somewhere we might still be found in, say, a 100 years or so. This, we think, would completely defeat the point of the exercise. In Sherwood Forest we feel certain that we will have a far less uncertain future.

I look forward to hearing from you in due course.

Yours truly,

Martin Endive (ex-BBC producer).

Forest Enterprise

An agency of the Forestry Commission

**Forest Enterprise
England**

**Sherwood and Lincs
Forest District**

Edwinstowe
Mansfield
Notts
NG21 9JL

Tel: 01623 822447
Fax: 01623 824975
E-Mail:
sherwood.fdo@forestry.gov.uk

Forest District Manager
Andy Medhurst

Mr M Endive
148 Montpelier Road
Brighton
East Susses
BN1 2LQ

Our Ref.

Dear Mr Endive

REGRESS SOCIETY ENQUIRY

Thank you for your letter and details of the Regress Society. I must say I am impressed with your group's determination to de-discover civilisation when most of us are content just to turn over in bed and put the pillow over our heads to escape society's vicissitudes. You assume that we do not receive letters like yours every day of the week. In one respect we do: where our correspondents have a complete misconception of the nature of Sherwood Forest.

Your obvious need is for a large area of undisturbed wilderness and this is one thing that Sherwood Forest has never had. With the other Royal Forests established in the late 12th century, Sherwood was designed for hunting game and comprised of open, heathy waste subject to Common and Forest Law. This open landscape persisted until the 19th Century by which time most of the old Royal Forest had passed into private hands. The woodlands within Sherwood today, apart from remnants close to Edwinstowe, in the north of the county, are modern plantations of relatively small size and excessively used for recreational access by the public. Not at all conducive to escaping the 21st century.

I regret that the Sherwood you envisage has as much substance as Tolkien's Middle Earth. Hollywood has much to answer for in this respect, as has television. As an ex-BBC producer, you should know all about that!

I am sorry to disappoint but strongly advise some serious exploration before you consider moving anywhere.

Yours sincerely

Paul Barwick
District Forester Environment
30 July 2004

Protecting and expanding Britain's forests and woodlands, and increasing their value to society and the environment.
Forest Enterprise is responsible for the management of forests and woodlands owned by the nation.
http://www.forestry.gov.uk

Alexander Literary, Film and Television Agency

148 Montpelier Road, Brighton, East Sussex, United Kingdom, BN1 2LQ.

Hotel Imperial,
1-1 Uchisaiwaicho 1-Chome,
Tokyo,
Japan.

Dear Sir or Madam,

I am writing to you as the managing director of the agency representing the 'British Snail Racing Federation'. The aforementioned federation has been a client of my agency for quite some time, and we have helped to arrange any number of racing venues for them, both in the UK and abroad.

They have recently asked me to investigate the possibility of them conducting a 'spectacular' snail race up the side of the Hotel Imperial - the highest building that they have ever used before being the Post Office Tower here in London. Let me explain a little of what would be involved.

The 'British Snail Racing Federation' uses only pedigree Madagascan snails in any of its races, and these snails, although quite capable of racing in the horizontal, are specifically trained to race in the vertical. Once a race has begun these 'Maddy's', as they are affectionately known, will continue to climb until they can climb no further, and the first one to the top is, of course, the winner.

We envisage that around ten of the fastest 'Maddy's' would be taking part in any such competition, and although groomed and attended in the final stages before any race, once they're out there on the side of the building they're on their own. Taking into account the height of the Imperial Hotel itself, we have calculated that the race winner will take between 54 – 68 hours to reach the finishing line.

During this time each competing snail would be monitored via a satellite-tracking device glued to his or her outer shell. This monitoring does not need to take place in the immediate vicinity of the building, and so would cause no inconvenience to you. All we would ask is that upon receiving information that a snail was about to triumph over his fellow competitors, we could be allowed access to the upper echelons of the Imperial Hotel in order to retrieve the victor. We would obviously need to leave someone up there in order to safely gather in those that come second, third, etc.

These races have been extraordinarily successful in the past and I am hoping that you can correspond with me as to your willingness to host such an event. We would be looking to run the race sometime over Easter 2005. Thank you for taking the time to consider this unusual request.

Yours truly,

Guy Piran.

IMPERIAL HOTEL
TOKYO

August 2nd, 2004

Mr. Guy Piran

Managing Director

Alexander Literary, Film and Television Agency

148 Montpelier Road

Brighton, East Sussex

BN1 2LQ

United Kingdom

Dear Mr. Piran,

We appreciate your letter of July 27th, which was routed to me for my attention and reply.

We find the idea of a Madagascar snail race absolutely charming, Mr. Piran, and have no doubt it would generate considerable publicity here in Japan. However, in view of the general character and mentality of our own market and guest make-up here, we do not feel The Imperial would be the most appropriate venue and hence wish to decline your offer. Nonetheless, we imagine you will easily find a venue here in Tokyo that will better suit the spirit of your races and hope you shall not be discouraged by our response.

Wishing you the best of luck with your plans, and with sincerest thanks for your having thought of The Imperial, I am

Yours sincerely,

Yasuhiro Maeda

Executive Director, Hotel Operations Management

YM/ic

148 Montpelier Rd,
Brighton,
East Sussex,
BN1 2LQ.

Brighton Sea Life Centre,
Marine Parade,
Brighton,
BN2 1TB

Dear Sir or Madam,

I am writing to you because my family and I now have a very big problem. When we bought 'Snickers' from the aquarium in Bristol three years ago he was entirely the size one would expect of your average sardine. We bought him as a present for my young son, Timothy, who has a keen interest in fish.

As he continued to grow we put it down to the fact that he was getting more food from us than he would normally have found in the wild. However, within a few months he had grown to such a length that we had to upgrade the fish tank to accommodate Snicker's burgeoning size. Some time later some of the smaller fish started to go missing, and then even some of the larger fish, such as the oriental carp, mysteriously disappeared.

Before too long we realised the awful truth, that our hitherto harmless sardine was devouring our complete fish stocks.

'Snickers' is now huge and living in our out-door pool. As you can imagine this is an inconvenience to my family and I, as I am not happy about even attempting to share the pool with a 200 pound sardine with an ever-increasing appetite.

Our neighbour, Mr Frank Hunter, has offered to harpoon 'Snickers' if we so wish but I do not really want any harm to come to him, let alone have to eat him for the next two years.

Would you have room in your aquarium for our heavyweight sardine? I am happy to help pay any expenses involved in having him shipped to you. If you are prepared to accept him I would suggest that you find him a place where he is not in any close proximity to smaller fish, unless they are fish that are well able to protect themselves from the umpteen rows of Snickers' razor-sharp teeth.

I do hope you can get back to me on this as soon as possible.

Yours truly,

G.K. Chesterton.

SEA·LIFE
—— BRIGHTON ——

THE MOST AMAZING, MOST WONDERFUL AQUARIUM IN THE WORLD.

Brighton Sea Life Centre, Marine Parade, Brighton, East Sussex BN2 1TB
Tel: 01273 604234 Fax: 01273 681840

Friday July 30th 2004

Dear GK Chesterton

Thank you for contacting us in respect of Snickers the giant sardine.

As you know, we at Sea Life are committed to protecting all aquatic creatures and where possible do endeavour to provide a home for oversized, injured or rescued fish. 'Orson' the Wells Catfish and 'Stumpy' the stingray are just two 'rescue' success stories at Brighton. Unfortunately, we simply do not have enough space to accommodate a sardine of Snickers' stature. At 200 pounds he is the size of an adult blue shark and requires a tank larger than anything available here.

Clearly, he cannot remain indefinitely in your swimming pool (which I'm assuming is saltwater hence Snickers continuing health). The Environment Agency has a team based in Kent that specialises in fish relocation. I suggest that you contact them as soon as possible. You may also consider approaching Guinness World of Records about your gargantuan pet since Snickers may qualify as a piscine record-breaker.

I trust the situation will soon improve for you, your family and fish. Meanwhile, perhaps a visit here may provide a brief respite for Timothy? To that end please find enclosed a complimentary family ticket to Brighton Sealife Centre.

Yours faithfully

Chris Burton
Entertainments Team Leader

PS. Are you perhaps related to your namesake the renowned man of letters and creator of Father Brown (1874-1936) ?

WEST MALLING GOD COLLECTIVE

148 Montpelier Road, Brighton, East Sussex, BN1 2LQ.

The Manager,
The Thistle Hotel,
King's Rd,
Brighton,
East Sussex.

Dear Sir or Madam,

I am writing to you as the acting Chairgod of the West Malling God Collective. Made up of nearly thirty-five Gods (both male and female), our collective came about through the inspirational divinity of the GrandGod himself, Arnold Pilkington. Arnold still rules us all from his suburban semi in West Malling, and even though we are all immortal, all-seeing, omnipotent and omniscient too, we defer to Arnold as the true progenitor of our Godliness and our ethereality.

We are hoping to have a get-together at your hotel during the second week of November 2004. We will be requiring rooms for all thirty-five Gods and their respective partners. Would you have an opening for that number of Gods and/or spouses at that time? We would also need to have the use of a reasonably large hospitality room that can hold all the Gods at any one time.

The reason that we're all getting together is so that we can all have a bash at creating the universe anew. To this end, would it be a further inconvenience to have all the bedroom suites close together on, for example, one floor of the hotel. Past experience has taught us that those unaware or ignorant of our Godlike doings (i.e. other guests at the hotel) often confuse the noise and clamour of our celestial doings, for more drunken and, perhaps, more *human* behavior

Actually, there really shouldn't be too much noise emanating from the individual chambers themselves. Where we do envisage there being a little more in the way of Big Bangs and Heavenly Vortices is when we will all be together for the Saturday nigh GodBash, which we would like to stage in the aforementioned hospitality suite. There really is no escaping the fact that 35 Gods in one room at any one time is an event of the highest magnitude, and excitement and exultation will no doubt be running high after a hard week of Universal Creation.

Would it also be possible for you to forward information relating to the leisure and entertainment facilities to be found at your establishment, as, although our Gods will be mostly pre-occupied whilst residing at the Grand, they do envisage having a relatively low-key and relaxing Sunday?

I should be most grateful if you could get back to me on the above matters and as to the availability of rooms at your prestigious establishment.

Yours truly,
God.

God
West Malling God Collective
148 Montpelier Road
Brighton
East Sussex, BN1 2LQ

Dear God

Thank you so much for considering our humble establishment for your proposed gathering of the 35-strong West Malling God Collective and respective partners.

It is with much regret that I have to advise you that our facilities do not extend to a hospitality room, although I would have thought that immortal, all-seeing, omnipotent and omniscient beings such as yourselves would already been aware of this. However, no-one is perfect, so I will allow your Great-ness this one small slip in your knowledge.

Much as I would like to have been involved in some small way in the re-creating of the universe (if only it was just to provide the location to do so) I feel that your request is one that is impossible for us to fulfil. This is, indeed, a great shame, because I feel that myself and my co-workers would benefit greatly from the Godlike energy surrounding the 35 Gods and Godesses, and we all admit to wondering what such a sight would look like - just imagine, 35 Gods/Goddesses wanting to reside at out establishment to carry out Celestial doings. As you say, exitement and exultation will be running very high after your week of Universal Creation, and that, again, is something that we would all like to see and be a part of.

I must admit, though, to feeling a little alarmed at the thought of the "Big Bangs and Heavenly Vortices" that I am told to expect at the Saturday night Godbash. I am not sure a building such as ours would be strong enough to withstand the aforementioned "Big Bangs and Heavenly Vortices", whatever they may be.

My final concern is the point you make regarding other guests possibly mistaking the above activities for more "drunken, human behaviour". I would estimate that at least 98% of our guests are human - I have my doubts about the remaining 2%, and as such, I think you are right to think that you would indeed be misunderstood.

Thank you so much for considering us for your gathering, and I wish you the best of luck in securing a suitable location.

Yours truly,
A N Other Human

148 Montpelier Rd,
Brighton,
East Sussex,
United Kingdom,
BN1 2LQ.

26.09.04

Jim Railton Auctioneers,
Nursery House,
Chatton,
Alnick,
Northumberland,
NE66 5PY

Dear Sir or Madam,

I am writing to you as I have recently come across an Item that I think is of unique historical value. I unearthed the object at a car boot sale here in Brighton, United Kingdom, where I paid a nominal price to someone who clearly had no idea what he was selling. I am now adamant that I have in my possession the complete genitalia of Rudolf Valentino. I can safely state this as I am a fluent Russian speaker and I have studied the accompanying corroborating literature closely (I think the man who sold them to me that cold and rainy day in Brighton will soon clearly rue the day that he did not speak Russian himself!).

Amongst the papers there is a signed affidavit from one of the custodians of the Hermitage Museum, one Alexander Andropov, signed and dated 1957. There is also a memorandum that appears to come from the KGB. The box within which the genitalia are housed also bears the remains of some sort of government seal, as does the linen bag within which the member is housed.

I should dearly like to know what such a commodity could raise at one of your auctions. Presumably you will have handled items not dissimilar to this in the past? My friend, who is a chiropodist, has had a good look at the entire package and he not only thinks that it would have come from a man of Valentino's age when he died, but also that it is in a condition which would be expected of a body part removed from a person in the year that Valentino actually did die.

Could you please get back to me as soon as possible? It would be no trouble for me to travel to your auction house for you to have a good look and give me a valuation. I look forward to hearing from you.

Yours truly,

Miriam Pankhurst

JIM RAILTON

ANTIQUES AUCTIONEER AND VALUER

Mrs Miriam Pankhurst
148 Montpelier Road
Brighton
East Sussex
BN1 2LQ

4 October 2004

Dear Mr Pankhurst,

Rudolf Valentino genetalia

Mr Tasker-Brown has passed me your letter of 26th September, as he thought I would be a suitable auctioneer to sell such an item. I have sold similar quirky items in the past, and it is really a matter of generating as much publicity as one can.

Obviously such pieces as yours do create a bit of stir, and I always feel such items always perform better "out in the sticks", rather than being sold in London. That way they can almost be 'discovered', and they get more attention/publicity, and hopefully a higher price as a result.

Obviously I would have to see the whole package which includes the box, the paperwork, the seals, etc. But I would advise a speculative estimate of £2000/£3000. However with such unique items, they really are impossible to predict value-wise, and it really is best to let such items find their own level, providing the marketing has been thorough. With the amount of editorial coverage an item like that would generate, it would require a good long lead-time to sell it to maximum advantage.

If you wish to proceed I would be delighted to handle the item for you, and I look forward to hearing from you in due course.

Yours,

P.S. Valentino was an Italian, so I cannot see what relevance russian is?

148 Montpelier Rd,
Brighton,
East Sussex,
BN1 2LQ.

Xenova Research Limited,
310 Cambridge Science Park,
Milton Road,
Cambridge,
CB4 0WG.

Dear Sir or Madam,

I am writing to complain most bitterly about a new anti-depressant that apparently is soon to come on the market. I have been told that this drug is called 'Ibinthrupain' and is to be issues to the general public in multi-coloured tablets that, to all intents and purposes, look just like 'Smarties'.

Are you entirely out of your pharmaceutical minds? I have never heard of anything more preposterous in all of my days! Further to this, my neighbour informs me that these tablets are to be contained in a dispenser, cylindrical in shape and just as multi-coloured as the tablets themselves.

My neighbour has suggested that this is all an attempt on your part to brighten up and prettify the taking of such drugs by depressed people. I hardly think that this is necessary whatsoever. People may be depressed, but they're not children.

I shudder to think of what you will come up with next – painkillers that look like Werthers Originals no doubt, or even suppositories in the shape of Mars Bars!

I should dearly like you to write back explaining your company policy and the 'reasoning' behind this quite ridiculous product.

I await your response with great interest.

Yours truly,

Miriam Gould. (Retired).

Xenova

www.xenova.co.uk

Xenova Research Limited
310 Cambridge Science Park, Cambridge, CB4 0WG, UK

Telephone: +44 (0)1223 423413
Facsimile: +44 (0)1223 423458

11th August 2004

Dear Miriam Gould,

With reference to your letter (attached) I understand your strong feelings regarding the pills that you have described looking like Smarties. Unfortunately, this is not one of our products. In fact we do not have any products on the market and we are certainly not developing any that look like Smarties.

I'm not sure exactly which company it is you hoped your letter would be sent to. There was once a company called Cantab Pharmaceuticals based on Cambridge Science Park which is now called Xenova. Cantab did not develop any pills like the ones you have described nor, in fact, did they have anything on the market. Millenium, I think, no longer has a site on the Cambridge Science Park.

I am sorry I cannot help you with this and wish you all the best in tracking down the correct company and I hope you reach a satisfactory conclusion to your complaint.

Yours sincerely,

Dr. Campbell Bunce

148 Montpelier Rd,
Brighton,
East Sussex,
BN1 2LQ.

Perth Zoo,
20 Labouchere Rd,
South Perth,
Western Australia,
6151

Dear Sir or Madam,

I am writing to you to offer my services. My name is Arthur Smitherington and I am a retired Steelworker from Scunthorpe. I am 62 and in good physical health with no congenital conditions whatsoever. I have receding grey hair, stand exactly six feet tall and I weigh 102 Kilos. I think I am a perfect example of your everyday, average, late-middle-aged Homo Sapien.

Would you consider finding room for me at your zoo? I have no objection to being put behind bars, even though this wouldn't really be necessary in terms of the public's safety- I'm not likely to bite anybody's hand!

In terms of accommodation, I would need a double bed, a wardrobe, a small chest of drawers and a small dining table. If there is room I would ideally like a two-seater sofa, but one easy chair will be sufficient if not.

My nutritional requirements will not cause you any difficulties. I like a traditional English breakfast, sandwiches for lunch, and meat and two veg for dinner. I am also more than happy to be fed crisps and other light refreshments from the visiting public - which would make a change from the prohibition zoos normally place on feeding the animals.

The aforementioned public will be able to watch me grooming myself in the morning, eating all my meals, reading the newspaper in the afternoon, and watching television in the early evening. I am also more than happy to entertain the crowd if necessary. I have a good repertoire of jokes and I can sing a number of Country and Western songs, although I wouldn't say that I sound exactly like Johnny Cash by any means.

If the zoo thought it a good idea I could also be a little mischievous as well. This could involve me stealing children's ice creams, shouting boo and making people jump, pretending to be doing something 'naughty' under the bedclothes. I could even pretend to be a monkey, and hop up and down making 'whooping' noises! That would really confuse the paying public.

I am not looking to be paid for coming to live and be displayed at your zoo (none of the other animals are, are they?). All I require is board and lodging. However, I have advertised in the national press for a female companion. I have received few replies as yet, but, with a bit of luck, it may be a possibility that you could end up with a male and a female Homo Sapien, which would make it much more interesting for everybody concerned. If she wasn't too old, we could even breed!

I really think that including me in your zoo will help to attract more paying visitors, and I'm sure you will attract local, perhaps even national news coverage which will be invaluable free publicity for you.

I look forward to hearing back from you.

Yours truly,

Arthur Smitherington.

PERTH ZOO

Mr Arthur Smitherington
148 Montpelier Road
Brighton
East Sussex
BN1 2LQ
UK

Dear Mr Smitherington

Thank you for your correspondence regarding your interest in being displayed at Perth Zoo.

Perth Zoo is particularly committed to the conservation and breeding of threatened and endangered species from the Australasian and African regions. As you will no doubt be aware, homosapians are presently far from being endangered in today's present society! Consequently, we do not have an interest in your kind offer.

I wish you the best of luck in sourcing a new home and also in finding a suitable mate.

Yours sincerely

Susan Hunt
Chief Executive Officer

3 August 2004

Tel (08) 9474 0444   Fax (08) 9474 4420   Email email@perthzoo.wa.gov.au   Web www.perthzoo.wa.gov.au
Address 20 Labouchere Road South Perth WA 6151 / PO Box 489 South Perth WA 6951

Susan Hunt,
Chief Executive Officer,
Perth Zoo,
20 Labouchere Road,
Perth,
WA 6151.

148 Montpelier Rd,
Brighton,
East Sussex,
United Kingdom,
BN1 2LQ

Dear Susan,

Thank you so much for your kind reply. I had no idea that Perth Zoo specialised in endangered species from the Australasian and African regions. If I'd known that then I wouldn't have applied in the first place. I must say I now feel a little foolish (a typical homo sapian character trait!).

I have, however, recently received hopeful news that a place may well have been found for me in a private zoo in Mexico City. All being well I should find myself being shipped there some time early in the New Year.

Unfortunately I have yet to source any kind of homo sapian mate. I would dearly like to rectify this situation as soon as possible, and I wonder if I might call upon your assistance in this matter. Would you be able to put up an advert for me in your zoo environs? Sometimes I feel a little endangered, and having a good mate around would certainly ease some of my irrational fears.

I've enclosed three posters (A4) for you to have a look at and, perhaps, use. I haven't included a phone number as I think this might attract 'cranks' and other undesirables. I want a mate that's prepared (and able!) to put homo sapian pen to paper, as it were. I'm not a homo erectus after all.

Thanks so much for considering my request.

Yours truly,

Arthur Smitherington.

WANTED

Large Homo Sapian Male Seeks Homo Sapian Female As Partner In Mexican Zoo Enterprise. Breeding Preferred And Must Be Accustomed to Restricted Environment.
No Pay But Most Necessities Accommodated.
Please Address Queries to:

Arthur Wesley Smitherington,
148 Montpelier Rd,
Brighton,
East Sussex,
United Kingdom,
BN1 2LQ.

Alexander Literary, Film and Television Agency

148 Montpelier Road, Brighton, East Sussex, United Kingdom, BN1 2LQ.

The Mayor of Brighton,
The Mayor's Office,
Bartholomew House,
Bartholomew Square,
Brighton,
BN1 1JP

Dear Sir or Madam,

I am writing to you as the Managing Director of the Alexander Agency. At present I represent clients throughout the entertainment industry, as well as chairing a number of charitable organizations. One of these charitable organizations is the Reformed Pick-pocket Association (RPA). Made up entirely of previous felons who now tread the paths of righteousness, the RPA boasts over 300 members who help to raise much needed funds by conducting street entertainment.

They are hoping that in May 2005 they will be able to bring their own particular blend of street theatre to Brighton in the hope of augmenting what will undoubtedly be a very exciting festival program.

What they have in mind is to be able to wander the streets of Brighton and Hove for an afternoon 'relieving' ignorant punters of their small change. All of these guy's are/were excellent pickpockets, and it would be very unlikely that anyone would be at all conscious of the fact that they will be being pick-pocketed. Furthermore, members of the RPA will only take small change and low denomination notes from the unsuspecting public. They will leave all wallets, purses, etc. on the body of the person being pick-pocketed, and interfere in no way with other valuables such as watches, chains or jewellery.

With the entire mobilization of the RPA we envisage that just permission to work the streets for two or three hours on a Saturday afternoon would be enough to raise quite considerable, and much needed funds.

I would be most grateful if you could get back to me on this matter as soon as possible as this performance would be one of several that we have planned for the forthcoming year, and this does take a good deal of organization. Furthermore, as something of a 'sweetener', the RPA would be more than willing to pay a percentage of the takings to Brighton Council as a kind of one-off license fee; and, as I have already indicated, 10% of all our projected charitable takings would not be an inconsiderable sum!

Thanks very much for taking the time to consider our proposal.

Yours truly,

Guy Piran.

BRIGHTON & HOVE CITY COUNCIL
THE MAYOR'S PARLOUR · TOWN HALL · BRIGHTON · BN1 1JA

Councillor Mrs. Pat Drake
Mayor

Mr. Guy Piran,
Alexander Literary, Film & Television Agency,
148 Montpelier Road,
Brighton, BN1 2LQ

Date: 30 July 2004

Ref: Mayor/PD

Dear Mr. Piran,

The Mayor of Brighton & Hove, Councillor Pat Drake, has asked me to write to thank you for your very interesting letter.

She has asked me to pass on your letter to Sue Drummond, Head of Leisure & Events, which I have done today.

Yours sincerely,

Pat Dines
Mayoral Secretary

West Chiltington Time-Travellers Cooperative
148 Montpelier Road, Brighton, East Sussex, BN1 2LQ.

Whytes Restaurant,
Brighton,
East Sussex

Dear Sir or Madam,

I am writing to you as the acting president of the West Chiltington Time-Travellers Cooperative. We would like to make an advanced booking for your restaurant for the evening of September 21st 2004.

Some of our party will be hoping to arrive long after the others, but most of us will be arriving long before anyone else. One or two will be popping in for a quick bite before going off and then coming back the day before the event is/was to have taken place. To that end, will it also be possible to make provisional booking for the evening of the 20th as well?

I myself will be there at the start to welcome everybody but then I'll be off, only to rejoin the restaurant in 2026 - that is, if the restaurant hasn't been closed down or turned into some sort of hideous theme park.

Incidentally, can you tell me when the restaurant first opened, as some of our members will be wishing to travel into the relatively distant past for dessert and/or coffee?

I'm sure that some of the above will throw up a few questions which you may want clearing up, so please do not hesitate to contact me with confirmation of our booking and any further clarification you seek.

Yours truly,

Arthur Askey.

John Anthony
4, Fairford Close
Haywards Heath,
W. Sussex RH16 3EF

Whytes Restaurant, Brighton

August 14, 2004

West Chiltington Time – Travellers Co op,
148 Montpelier Road, Brighton
Attention: Mr Askey

Dear Arthur,

Thank you for your recent request for a booking on 21st September.

Unfortunately we are full on that particular evening. As you probably aware, Brighton is hosting the X11th Centennial Klingon Cultural Sensitivity and War Games convention during that week and we will be very busy. I doubt if you'd want to share – they can get pretty ugly after a couple of Pan Galactic Gargle Blasters and the Interstellar wake of their warp drives would probably bugger up your navigation systems. Keeping food hot for an extra millennia is a real problem.

The following week is no better, I'm afraid. There are a lot of "back to skool" events hosted by the Brighton Independent Group of Transsexual Impersonators & Transvestites ("BIGTITS") who have, for obvious reasons, demanded sole occupancy of our humble emporium for the duration.

I'm delighted, however, that news of our culinary abilities has reached Galifree. I have taken the liberty of enclosing a menu of a meal the good Doctor enjoyed on his one failed mission – saving the Titanic – which may, perhaps, offer the theme for a good bash next April. I'm sure the esteemed Henry Butler, of Butlers wine lodge, would be happy to suggest a suitable '95 Claret (1895, that is).

Yours sincerely,

John Anthony
(Ex Proprietor)

Alexander Literary, Film and Television Agency

148 Montpelier Road, Brighton, East Sussex, United Kingdom, BN1 2LQ.

Events Organiser,
Brighton Pier,
Madeira Drive,
Brighton,
East Sussex,
BN2 1TW

Dear Sir or Madam,

I am writing to you as the managing director of the Alexander Literary, Film and Television Agency here in Brighton. Along with interests in contemporary Entertainment, we also act as agents for a number of societies and charities, helping to organise events and functions. One of our long-established client organisations has recently been in touch with us as to the feasibility of hosting a particular event. It is with this in mind that I am writing to you in this particular instance.

The 'We're in Control Even Though We Look Like We're Out Of Control Co-- operative' boasts a steady and increasing membership and are seeking to conduct a number of fundraising events in 2004. They would like to know whether they would be able to hire some or all of the Palace Pier on a Saturday in September for about 200 of the societies members. I have actually been to one of their events before and I can assure you that it was an extremely memorable experience, and that was only a small- scale affair for 30 members held at a country farm near Steyning. I can't even imagine what 200 members of this society on Palace Pier will be like but, though I can't be there myself, I'll definitely try to get someone to shoot some video.

They are not concerned whether or not all the entertainment facilities are available in September (it being off-season), but they would hope that some of the end-of-pier mechanical rides are in operation. Would karaoke also be available in one of your bars? Also, could you tell me if the Palace Pier has a policy about running on the pier. I have to say I have never seen any signs saying explicitly 'no running' . I would definitely need clarification on this before we could go ahead with any booking arrangements.

Also would you happen to know off-hand the distance between the end-of-pier side railings and the sea below? Presumably this varies according to the tides?

I should be most grateful if you could write back to my agency with the information requested above, and to suggest any dates in September 2004 when this particular co- operative could be accommodated.

Yours truly,

Guy Piran.

Guy Piran
Alexander Literary Film and TV Agency
148 Montpelier Road
Brighton
BN1 2LQ

Dear Guy

Please find enclosed our Wedding and Corporate Event Brochure.

Brighton Pier holds functions from September to May, Monday to Friday; excluding school and Bank holidays. We have four venues for exclusive hire and can cater for 60-350 people. Room hire is charged extra and is dependent on variables such as chosen date, venue, numbers in party and menu options, please enquire for more details.

The Pleasuredome Arcade can be hired on an hourly basis for your guests to play free of charge. We can pre arrange wrist bands with unlimited access to the rides or pre paid game tickets.

If you would like to view the venues and discuss your event further, please call to make an appointment or to have an informal chat. I look forward to hearing from you and thank you for your interest in Brighton Pier.

Yours sincerely

Susana Mascarenhas
Pr & Marketing
Brighton Pier

Brighton Marine Palace & Pier Company Madeira Drive, Brighton, East Sussex BN2 1TW
T: +44 (0) 1273 609361 F: +44 (0) 1273 684289 E: info@brightonpier.co.uk W: www.brightonpier.co.uk
Registered Office: 45 Cuthbert Court, Bede Industrial Estate, Jarrow, Tyne & Wear, NE32 3HG. Registered in England & Wales No: ZC164

Polo,
Nestle UK Head Office,
Nestle UK Ltd,
St George's House,
Croydon,
Surrey,
CR9 1NR

Dear Sir or Madam,

I am writing to you over what I consider to be a very serious matter indeed. For many years now I have made use of your Polo product, enjoying its unique minty flavour. You have many competitors with what are considered to be 'similar' products, but none have been a match for Polo. Imagine my disgust, then, to discover that you have been defrauding the sweet-buying public. How do I know this? I shall tell you.

Last week, while searching through my wardrobe I came across an old coat that I haven't worn for many, many years. I put it to one side with the intention of dropping it off at the Oxfam shop on my next visit. Without really thinking I checked the pockets. I am normally very assiduous about not leaving things in pockets, so it is very unusual for me to check pockets at all.

However, and to my astonishment, I pulled forth an unopened packet of Polo's. These Polo's are at least twenty years old, and possibly a good deal older. With trepidation I opened the packet and loosened one of the sweets. Because of the temperate conditions within which these Polo's had been stored the sweets themselves were in near-perfect condition (I have never doubted that Polo use only the finest ingredients in their manufacturing process).

I slipped the Polo into my mouth and followed my customary procedure of rolling the Polo around my mouth several times, before finally investigating the inimitable hole with the tip of my tongue. After a little gentle tonguing, I became concerned that my tongue could not penetrate the hole as much as it is normally capable of doing. For comparison I tried another Polo and got similar results. I wondered if my tongue had somehow become swollen or enlarged, but then I remembered that I had a new packet of Polo's in the downstairs bureau drawer that I had bought but the day before.

I raced down the stairs and within moments I had an 'old' Polo in my left cheek and a 'new' one in my right. A few moments later I knew Polo's dark and sordid truth: the hole in the new Polo is considerably bigger than in the 'old' variety. How very clever of you. Ostensibly people are buying exactly the same size packet of Polo's only what they don't realise is that inside there's a whole lot more hole than there used to be.

I have now taken the 'old' Polo's and deposited them with my bank for safekeeping. And what I would like to know now is if Polo are going to have the decency to come clean about their enlarged holes? Believe me, if and when this goes to the press there will no doubt be international outrage. I should imagine that a number of life-long supporters such as myself might jump ship and take up with Trebor or Spears. And then where will your product margins and profits be?

I would like to know in writing just what you intend to do about this deplorable situation. And don't think you can buy me off with a few free boxes of your product. This lady's not got a price on her head.

I look forward to hearing from you forthwith.

Yours truly,

Edna Pilkington.

Nestlé UK Ltd

YORK YO91 1XY

Telephone 01904 604604
Facsimile 01904 604534

Register with Nestlé for the latest
product news & special offers
www.nestle.co.uk

Ms E Pilkington
148 Montpelier Road
BRIGHTON
East Sussex
BN1 2LQ

DATE:

DIRECT LINE: 0800 000030

DIRECT FAX: 01904 603461

1337322A   4 August 2004

Dear Ms Pilkington

Thank you for your recent letter concerning Polo Mints.

The holes in Polo mints have neither reduced nor enlarged, they have stayed the same since the outset in 1948.

Hope this satisfies your query.

Yours sincerely

Joel Hancocks
Senior Supervisor
Consumer Services

148 Montpelier Rd,
Brighton,
East Sussex,
BN1 2LQ.

Gardenvista,
6 Kingsbury Rd,
Brighton,
East Sussex,
BN1 4JR

Dear Sir or Madam,

I am writing to you in the hope that you may be able to help me redesign my garden. At present I lead a very busy life and I have been able to devote only a small amount of my time to the upkeep of this garden. For this reason my garden is now in need of attention, and I think it is time to bring in the professionals.

My garden is a bonsai garden that measures 12 inches by 14 inches. The mainstay of the garden is a sycamore tree that is seven inches high and planted on a rocky outcrop. The borders of the garden are made up of miniature grasses and mosses, which are now several millimetres higher than they should be.

I have had a discussion with my partner and we would like to now add some new features to our garden. Do you have any experience at installing water features? We would dearly like to have a lotus pond installed with a small stream leading down to a pagoda. We would like this stream to be bordered by rose bushes and bull-rushes. We would also like some electrical lighting features so as to best show off the garden at night.

At present we do not have any area of plain lawn, and we would dearly like to have a designated area flattened and re-turfed. Our children, Emily and John, would also like to have a tree house erected in the aforementioned sycamore tree if you think this possible.

I guess that the best thing would be for you to come round and take a look at our garden with a view to giving us a quote for the work mentioned above. I very much look forward to hearing from you soon.

Yours truly,

Mrs Teresa Borrower.

GARDENVISTA

DESIGN · CONSTRUCTION · RESTORATION

29-7-2004

148 Montpelier Rd,
Brighton,
East Sussex
BN1 2LQ

Dear Mrs. Borrower

GardenVista would be pleased to help you redesign and build your garden, to this end a site visit would be necessary, in order to accurately measure and assess the plot. We at GardenVista have the most up to date surveying equipment, Laser levels and theodolites will be used to map the topography, we will also incorporate a state of the art satellite mapping system similar to the one used by NASA, for the Mars and lunar landings. We can also, at a small cost, call upon the services of the BBC Time Team to do a geophysical survey, in order that we may be able to avoid disturbing any valuable archeological remains that may be lurking under your garden.

WATER FEATURE
GardenVista is well versed in the supply and installation of all of all types of water features, we have in stock at the moment a 'new to the market' 'Thimble' pond, this pond can be installed either with, or without, its own miniature stream, this item comes complete with its own built in bull- rushes (Moses basket optional) and rose bushes, I am pleased to say that the roses are a variety that are particularly well suited when planted near water, as they are hardy to both powdery mildew and rose rust. You could also plump for the 'Delux' version, complete with water filter and infrared microbiological algae destroyer.

LIGHTING
As for electrical lighting, we can supply an eco friendly alternative to the 'common or garden' (excuse the pun) lighting at present available on the market, namely, 'Glow worms'.
These can be trained to sit in the most advantageous place to suit your requirements, for example, if you are sitting under your Sycamore tree at night, having a read, you only have to ask a few of them to crawl up into the tree to provide all your lighting requirements. The added advantage of these little creatures is that they do not need to be fed, as they eat grass, this will save you the bother of having to cut your lawn, or for that matter having to buy a lawn mower, or a shed to store it in!

Telephone Andrew John Forsey on Btn 01273 706213 or 07710 661944, 6 Kingsbury road, Brighton, East Sussex BN1 4
E-mail to: mrvista@tinyonline.co.uk
www.gardenvista.co.uk

PRINTED ON RECYCLED PAPER

GARDENVISTA
DESIGN · CONSTRUCTION · RESTORATION.

LAWN

We can supply and lay a wide variety of lawn types, as there is the possibility that your Sycamore tree will produce a significant amount of shade in your garden, it is suggested that we supply a variety of turf called 'shade lawn' you should find that this will survive where other types would normally die off, it also has the advantage of being extremely hard wearing, so when Emily and John become huge galumphing teenagers, the lawn will be able to take the strain. However it must be pointed out to them that size nine shoes and feeding Glowworms are a bad mix.

TREE HOUSE

At the present time we are unable to say whether it would be possible to erect a tree house in the aforementioned Sycamore tree. This due to the fact that we would need to visit with our tree surgeon, he would then be able to scale the tree, and inspect it. A full report as to the state of the tree would then be produced. I have to say that I have my doubts as to the suitability, due to the inherent shallow roots that this species has.

I trust that I have covered the salient points of your letter, and await your reply so that we can meet on site and take matter further.

Yours truly,

Alan Tich mouse.

PP Garden Vista

elephone Andrew John Forsey on Btn 01273 706213 or 07710 661944; 6 Kingsbury road, Brighton, East Sussex BN1 4JR
E-mail to: mrvista@tinyonline.co.uk
www.gardenvista.co.uk

PRINTED ON RECYCLED PAPER

148 Montpelier Rd,
Brighton,
East Sussex,
BN1 2LQ.

Going Places Travel Agency,
42 George Street,
Hove,
East Sussex,
BN3 3YB

Dear Sir or Madam,

I am writing to you as the widow of the late Jonathan Lloyd-Margoyles. My husband died in August of this year from complications following what should have been a routine foot operation. His tragic loss has left our family devastated. He was in the prime of his life and we both had so much to look forward to.

When Jonathan and I were first married and before we had children we had planned to go round the world together. Unfortunately, life being what it is, we never made that trip, but we promised ourselves that when the children were all grown up we would fulfil this shared dream of ours. That will never be the case now, and that makes me very sad.

However, Toby, who is seven, came to me the other day and told me he had a plan for Daddy, which he thought would make me happy. Toby has been hit very hard by the loss of his father, but he has been equally concerned and upset by my evident sadness. He then told me his extraordinary plan, and I could not believe that a seven-year-old could be so ingenious. That is why I am writing to you now.

Would it be possible for your travel company to organise a round-the-world ticket for my late husband Jonathan? We have his ashes in a silver tureen that has now been sealed with solder. I know this must seem like an extraordinary requestl, but the more my family have thought about it, the more enthusiastic we have become with the idea. As Toby says, it would be like giving daddy one last great adventure - not only that but it would be fulfilling a lifelong wish of his.

Would it be possible for you to organise this? For obvious reasons my late husband would not need to spend any great length of time at particular places before moving on to forward destinations. With this in mind we envisage that his whole trip may only last a few weeks at the most. Presumably Jonathan wouldn't need a passport and, because of the sealed nature of his urn he wouldn't need to be 'declared' at every check-in. I know with present terrorist threats around the world that airline security has been stepped-up considerably, but one good X-Ray will be more than sufficient to indicate that Jonathan is not a bomb.

If you are capable of accommodating us then perhaps you could send us a list of destinations with pricing formats for different combinations of stops. I think the family and I will have a great deal of fun deciding exactly where Jonathan will travel to on his final trip.

Also, could you include in your correspondence details of specific insurance packages? We are not worried in the slightest about the silver tureen, but it would undoubtedly be a double tragedy if my family and I were to lose Jonathan for a second time.

I look forward to hearing back from you soon.

Yours truly,

Miriam Lloyd-Margoyles.

Going Places

42 GEORGE STREET
HOVE
E.SUSSEX
BN3 3YB

0870 8530248
30 Jul 2004

Mrs M Lloyd-Margoyles
148 Montpelier Road
Brighton
East Sussex
BN1 2LQ

Dear   Mrs Lloyd-Margoyles

Re:

Firstly, may I say how sorry we were to learn of your recent loss.

We would be very happy to give you all the assistance you may need to arrange a round the world trip for your husband, however we need a few more details in order to give you an idea of cost and itinerary.

The details that we need are as follows:

How many people will be accompanying your husband?
Are there any places that you or your husband particularly want to travel to?
When would you be thinking of taking the trip?
Will you require accommodation at the places you visit?

Please contact us with this information so that we can start to put together an itinerary for you.

Yours faithfully

Travel Adviser

148 Montpelier Rd,
Brighton,
BN1 2LQ

Going Places,
42 George Street,
Hove,
East Sussex.

1.09.04

Dear Sir or Madam,

Thank you so much for your prompt response to my letter of enquiry of the 27th July. I must apologise for not getting back to you sooner, but my family and I have been away on our annual August holiday.

I am entirely delighted that you feel able to arrange a round the world trip for my late husband. Let me now provide you with the further details you requested.

There will be one other person travelling with my husband's sealed urn, though as yet we haven't decided who that will be.

In terms of any itinerary, we would like to go round the world from east to west. Therefore Jonathan's first projected stop will be the USA. I'm sure he'd love to spend a few nights in New York City before heading across the states on an internal flight to Las Vegas. We envisage spending a night or two in Las Vegas before heading south to Acapulco in Mexico.

The projected Itinerary from there will be roughly as follows:

Acapulco to Bogota
Bogota to Brazilia
Brazilia to Tonga
Tonga to Auckland
Auckland to Sydney
Sydney to Bangkok
Bangkok to Kathmandu
Kathmadu to Moskow
Moskow to London Heathrow

Jonathan and his 'carrier' will be spending more time in some places than others, but wherever we do stay we will be arranging separate accommodation ourselves.

Jonathan will require his own seat throughout the round-the-world trip, as we don't want to compromise his dignity by having him sitting in somebody's lap all the time.

I hope the above information will be sufficient for you to give us a reasonable approximation of projected costs. Would it also be possible for you to provide us with a quote for travel insurance – we dearly want to ensure Jonathan's safe return!

Yours truly,

Miriam Lloyd-Margoyles.

42 George Street
Hove
East Sussex
BN3 3YB

Mrs Lloyd-Margoyles
148 Montpelier Road
Brighton
BN1 2LQ

17/09/2004

Dear Mrs Lloyd-Margoyles

Thankyou for your letter dated 01/09/2004.

I have been working with my flight department to put together some costings and establish each airlines rules with regards to carrying your husband on board the aircraft and to get some costings for the routing you have given me.

As the routing is quite complex it will involve flying with seven different airlines. We have explained your situation to these airlines and there is not a problem with your husband occupying a seat, however Air New Zealand have advised that he cannot be visible and so would need to be carried in something that would conceal him from other passengers. All the other airlines are fine with your husband occupying a seat. They would need a letter from the crematorium confirming the contents of the urn and the urn would need to be x-rayed at the airports.

You did not advise in your letter at what time of year you would be hoping to take this trip so I have based costings on January to give you an idea, however if you would like prices for other times of the year please advise me and I would be happy to get a cost for you. Please bear in mind that flights in December will probably be quite limited on availabilty due to the peak christmas season.

The cost that I have been given is approximately £3270 per person for the itinerary you have given me. I am waiting to hear from the insurance company to make sure they can cover your husband and as soon as I have a quote for this I will let you know.

Yours faithfully

Georgina Porter
Travel Adviser

148 Montpelier Rd,
Brighton,
East Sussex,
BN1 2LQ.

Ebenezer Baptist Chapel,
Richmond Parade,
Brighton,
East Sussex

Dear Sir or Madam,

I am writing to you in exasperation. I have already approached a number of other parish priests with the wish for them to perform a christening service for my quadruplet children. Both my wife and I have been practising Christians all our lives and we wish for our four boys to grow up within the bosom of the church too. It is therefore very important that our children are christened as soon as possible (they are all now approaching two).

The reason we have been refused by the other parishes stems entirely from what we have chosen to call our children. Let me provide you with their full names: John Gordon Lucifer Sumner-Stanger, Luke Jack Lucifer Sumner-Stanger, Ricky Lucifer Charles Edward Sumner-Stanger, and finally Django Angelo Lucifer Sumner-Stanger. We understand how certain priests might view the middle name 'Lucifer' in the wrong light. It is certainly a name which has been abused somewhat. But my wife and I have chosen this name carefully and view it in entirely Old Testament terms where it signifies 'light bringer'.

Our four beautiful children have brought a good deal of light into both our lives and we really cannot see why such an appropriate name cannot be used at their combined christening.

Would it be possible for you to get back to me on this as soon as you are able, and if you feel you are not able to conduct such a service perhaps you could explain your reasons why without slipping into the superstitious, which a number of the other priests have done.

I look forward to your reply,

Yours truly,

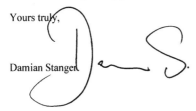

Damian Stanger

Pastor Tony Bickley,
18, Sadler Way,
Brighton,
BN2:5PL.   01273:674453.   9/8/04.

Dear Mr. Stanger,

In response to your request about the Christening of you four children, the first problem that we face is the fact that I am the minister of a Baptist Church, and Baptist Churches do not Christen, they baptize only those who have made a profession of faith in Jesus Christ at an age where they are able to understand both the faith they profess, and what the consequences of that profession mean to their lives. We do whoever dedicate children, this mean that we give them to the Lord and make promises to bring them up in the way of the Lord and according to the Word of God. It is on the point of the Word of God that I will address the rest of this letter.

The first thing that I notice is that you call me a priest, from this it would seem that you are either of Catholic or high Anglican background. The Bible teaches us that there is no priest hood in the New Testament Church. The priesthood of the Old Testament was a picture of He who was to come into the world and who would stand in the gap between mankind and His Father in heaven; they speak of the Lord Jesus Christ who is our High Priest and our only priest. The work of priesthood is to stand between the people and God and to represent them in heaven. The Lord Jesus Christ alone can do this, and the Old Testament priesthood only foreshadowed the event of His life and death and eventual ascension into heaven. The picture held here is one of representation or advocacy, and if you look up the words priest and advocate in the New Testament you will find that all favorable references to this office are attributed to the Lord Jesus Christ. The ministers of the Church are called pastors, or sometimes bishops, and their role is not to stand between the people and present them to God, but it is one of oversight and instruction, just as a shepherd would care for his sheep, the Lord Jesus Christ being the chief of the Shepherds.

The second issue I would bring to your attention is the fact that you say that you are practicing Christians, I would like to know where you practice your Christianity, what Church you attend, and if you do not attend any Church, or if you attend a Church in error, then I would ask why this is. The Bible speaks to us of *not forsaking the gathering together of the saints,* just as it tells us that we must *worship in spirit and in truth.* To worship the Lord in *Spirit and in Truth,* you must first be *born again of the Spirit of God,* and then worship Him according to the truth of His Word; I await your reply on this matter.

Finally the naming of your children, I find it strange that you would want to associate your children with one of the names of he who became Satan, or the Devil. Where it is true that the literal translation of the name Lucifer is *brightness,* the root word from which it is taken means much more. The Hebrew word is *halal,* pronounced **haw-lal.** It means such things as to shine, but it means it in the sense of making a show, or boasting, and thus to be clamorous or foolish. It means to rave, to celebrate, to stultify, to boast, to glory in oneself rather in God. By this meaning you can see why it was the name given to the Angel of heaven who would fall through pride and boasting. I cannot think that you would want to name your children in such a way, let alone have them carry a name that is so associated with the evil one. It was the name of Satan before his fall, but it was a name that explains to us the cause of his fall.

If you could answer my questions with regards to your own spiritual condition, I would be pleased to come and discus with you the subject of a dedication service. I am certain that if you truly love the Lord more than your own selves, you will see the inconvenience that you will place upon your children by naming them in such a way. I have enclosed a booklet that might help you to understand where you are spiritually, and I await your reply with interest.

Yours sincerely,

A. R. Bickley   Pastor of Ebenezer Baptist Chapel,
                 Richmond Parade,
                 Brighton.

148 Montpelier Rd,
Brighton,
East Sussex,
BN1 2LQ.

Gamleys,
Unit 86, Lower Level,
Churchill Square,
Brighton,
East Sussex,
BN1 2TF.

Dear Sir or Madam,

I am writing to you because an associate of mine has told me that you have in stock a very exciting product - namely the walking/talking Kylie Minogue doll. Does this doll really look just like Kylie Minogue? My associate tells me that it is the spitting image, right down to the perky little nose. My associate also informs me that this doll not only walks and talks but can do other things too. Could you give me some indication as these other functions? For example, I am informed that it might have functioning 'front' and 'back' bottoms. Is this the case? If this is true are they realistic looking and how are they properly maintained?

I am obviously not interested in acquiring this doll for myself. It would be a present for somebody I know. That is why I would like to make sure about all of its functioning capabilities right from the start - just so that it would be right for the person I am thinking of giving it to.

Are there also different outfits that you can buy for the doll. Again, I am led to believe that a good deal of the costumes that the real Kylie wears in videos may be available for the doll too. Does this include underwear? If I were to buy a few Kylie Dolls would I get a reduction, especially if I buy all of the clothing available with the product?

I would be most grateful if you could write back to me with answers to my questions and as to whether you would have a number of Kylies available. When you do write back could you do so using a plain envelope as I would not like my wife to know what I am doing. It would certainly spoil any surprise !

Thank you for your time in considering this matter.

Yours truly,

Arthur Rumptonn

Gamleys Limited
Unit 68, Lower Level
Churchill Square
Brighton
BN1 2TF

Tel: 01273 329675

e-mail: brighton@gamleys.co.uk

03 August 2004

148 Montpelier rd,
Brighton,
East Sussex,
BN1 2LO.

Dear Arthur Rumpton,

In response to your inquiry about the Kylie doll, your associate was correct, we do stock the Kylie doll and I think it does look like the real thing even down to her perky little nose. Unfortunately she doesn't walk and talk and has no functioning front or back bottoms. I think if she did have functioning front and back bottoms I don't what you could do with them, as she is only 12" tall. We stock two types of dolls one in the silver Dolce & Gabbana outfit and one in the red Dolce & Gabbana outfit that she wore at the world music awards. I have heard of there being extra outfits available but we do not stock them, but I haven't heard of extra underwear for the doll. As any Kylie fan would know though, you can get adult underwear in Selfridges in London all designed by Kylie herself.

Yours faithfully
for and on behalf of Gamleys Limited

Lee Ward
Store Manager

The Manager,
Grosvenor Casino,
Albany Mews,
Fourth Avenue,
Hove
BN3 2PQ

Dear Sir or Madam,

I am writing to you as the head of the Brighton and Hove Dangerous Odds Club. We specialise in taking risks and gambling where others fear to tread. For example, each one of our club members, including myself, individually bet £100 pounds on Red Rum winning the 2003 Grand National. Unquestionably we lost, but we felt glorious in our defeat. For us it's not the winning that counts but the excitement of taking part - especially when the odds are stacked against us.

To this end, would it be possible for our club members to visit you casino for an evening, and would you have a roulette table and 21's table for the use of our club members only? The reason we ask this is because we would not want to conflict with ordinary low-odds gamblers.

Given that the above is forthcoming we would then like to specify that the only number on the roulette wheel that we could use to bet on would be the number 7. All other usual betting on the table would be suspended, with the winning odds remaining the same for that specific number. As you can imagine this drastically cuts down the winning chances of our club members, but let me assure you it will most certainly greatly increase their collective thrill.

As regards the 21's table the only hand that our club members will be able to stick on is 21 itself. We think this also greatly increases the odds in your favour.

None of our club members are exactly millionaires but you can probably expect them to bring to the casino what your average punter would bring (perhaps a thousand or two).

We would need no further special provision to be made, and we hope that you feel able to entertain us in our self-imposed high-odds pursuits. I look forward to hearing from you in due course.

Yours truly,

Guy Piran.

GROSVENOR CASINO
ALBANY MEWS
28 FOURTH AVENUE
HOVE BN3 2PQ
TELEPHONE 01273 720261
FACSIMILE 01273 734863

Mr. Guy Piran
148 Montpelier Road
Brighton
East Sussex
BN1 2LQ

2nd August 2004

Dear Mr. Piran,

Thank you very much for your letter regarding a visit to our Club.

Could you please contact me on the above telephone number to discuss your proposals.

Yours sincerely

B. T. Fox

Brenda T. Fox
General Manager

148 Montpelier Rd,
Brighton,
East Sussex,
BN1 2LQ.

Specialist Precast Products Ltd,
Pant Glas Industrial Estate,
Bedwas Gwent,
NP1 8DR

Dear Sir or Madam,

I am writing to get a quote for a number of concrete items that I'd like to have made. I'd like a batch of twenty concrete blocks made up measuring approximately 70cm by 70cm. I need all the blocks to have an opening on one side large enough to fit a foot and lower leg. Do you have the facility to manufacture such a product? I also need to know whether you consider that any such block will be of a weight that, for example, a couple of well-built chaps could lift?

Would you also be able to provide an amount of quick-setting concrete mix that can be used to 'plug-up' the aforementioned openings?

I would be most grateful if you could get back to me on this as soon as possible, as I need to make use of these concrete blocks in the near future.

Yours truly,

Frankie Richardson.

QUOTATION

Your Ref

Our Ref **MEF. 24 - 8/14**

FRANKIE RICHARDSON.
148, MONTPELIER RD,
BRIGHTON,
EAST SUSEX
BN1 2LP.

**SPECIALIST
PRECAST
PRODUCTS**

Pant Glas Industrial Estate
Bedwas Gwent NP1 8DR
02920
Tel 880800
Fax 880700

Dear Sir(s). We thank you for your recent enquiry and have pleasure in submitting our prices which we trust will receive your favourable consideration.

RE CONCRETE BLOCKS C40 - CONCRETE 6.

20# 700 x 700 x 700.   ① £486.00 EACH

    (OPENING 300 x 300 x 600)
WAIGHT / BLCC. 640KG APPROX.

APPROX 8 WEEK TO MANUFACTURE

Delivered To **EX WORKS**

Owing to continually rising costs in Labour and Materials we are unable
to quote fixed prices (refer to General Conditions item 2, overleaf).

SPECIALIST PRECAST PRODUCTS LTD

Delivery **£295.20/LOAD**

Terms DEPOSIT 33⅓%
BALANCE PRONTO
DELL

Yours faithfully

M E for

Warwick Tourist Information Centre,
Court House,
Jury Street,
Warwick,
CV34 4EW

Dear Sir or Madam,

I am writing to you to ascertain a few things about what you may or may not be able to offer me. At some point in the near future I am going to be in need of some information, and I want to ensure that I know beforehand if this information is going to be forthcoming from yourselves. For example, how much general information do you have? Is this information general in the broadest sense, or does it have some specifics that make it less general?

With regard to specific information, is this information accessed via an indexed system? If this is the case, how specific does this information have to be to be included in any such database? Does this database exclude certain specific and detailed areas of information, because they may have been deemed in the past to have had little or no relevance to customer queries? I sometimes find that this 'excluded' and overlooked specific information is just what I'm looking for. Could you also indicate if there are any general areas of information that you exclude for similar reasons to the 'excluded' specific information?

If I was to visit your offices how much information would I be able to take away with me? I am not brilliant, I have to say, at storing information in terms of my memory. My memory has let me down on occasion, and I have not been able to retrieve precious bits of information. Once or twice this has proved to be quite injurious to my health!

If you can help me with the above queries I would be most grateful, and I look forward to hearing from you in the near future.

Yours truly,

Stewart Potts.

Warwick Tourist Information Centre

The Court House, Jury Street, Warwick CV34 4EW
Tel: 01926 492212 Fax: 01926 494837
E-mail: touristinfo@warwick-uk.co.uk

July 2004

ewart Potts
8 Montpelier Road
ghton
st Sussex
1 2LQ

ar Stewart

ank you for your letter. This Tourist Information Centre operates a holiday information service and we do ep information on the whole of the United Kingdom and we do keep a list of all brochures in stock. It is ssible to take this information away with you free of charge (we do also sell some guide books which you ght find useful). I would suggest that you telephone our office to check that we have specific information avoid disappointment.

ope this has helped.

urs sincerely

son Rowberry

Alexander Literary, Film and Television Agency

148 Montpelier Road, Brighton, East Sussex, United Kingdom, BN1 2LQ.

General Enquiries,
City Hall,
The Queen's Walk,
London,
SE1 2AA

Dear Sir or Madam,

I am writing to you as the managing director of the Alexander Literary, Film and Television Agency. I have recently taken on a new client who has only recently arrived in the UK from Hong Kong. Ang Sho Lee is an acclaimed performance artist and famous throughout the Chinese-speaking world for his inspirational, improvised performances.

Ang would like to garner permission from you to perform some of his inspired theatre in and around some famous London landmarks. He will be performing under his theatrical name of Mousy Tongue.

For example, he would like to perform in Trafalgar Square. This would be where he appears as a customary Chinese tourist. He will walk around Trafalgar Square admiring Nelson's Column and then take some photographs of the pigeons. He will then put out his arm and allow some of the birds to perch there for a few moments. Ang envisages the whole performance taking little more than twenty-five minutes.

Ang would also like to stand outside the gates of Buckingham Palace, again in his tourist persona. He will stare through the closed gates for about 10 minutes and smile at passers by.

As part of his theatrical repertoire would it also be possible for Ang to perform directly outside the Houses of Parliament? He would be sitting on a conveniently placed park bench and eating his lunch, which will consist of an over-priced small bottle of water, an over-priced and thoroughly inedible sandwich, and an apple with very few distinguishing characteristics.

Even though Ang sees this latter performance as being one of the highlights of his street theatre, he does not see it lasting much over twenty minutes.

As a finale to his weekend extravaganza Ang would then like to do on the spot improvisations lasting a few seconds only. This he would like to do down the length of Oxford Street. One minute he'll be walking like any other tourist and the next minute he'll have stopped outside a shop window. He will look at certain items through the window and, on occasion, he will point at something before rapidly moving on. This final 'assemblage' of miniature performances he envisages taking anywhere between two to three hours, depending upon the crowds.

Will Ang have to apply for a special permit for any of the above, and if so how much is this going to cost? Ang does envisage some indoor theatre (staring at pictures in the National Gallery, watching the Phantom of the Opera, shopping at Harrods) and we shall be contacting the requisite parties for permission for these additional performances.

If you could contact my agency with your response to our requests I would be most grateful.

Yours truly,

Guy Piran.

City Hall
The Queen's Walk
London SE1 2AA
Switchboard: 020 7983 4000
Minicom: 020 7983 4458
Web: www.london.gov.uk

Our ref: MGLA260804-7348
Your ref:
Date: 01 September 2004

Guy Piran
Alexandra Literary, Film and Television Agency
148 Montpelier Road
Brighton BN1 2LQ

Dear Mr Piran,

Thank you for your letter to the Mayor of London, which has been passed on to me for a response.

For any event proposed by an organisation there is an application process to use the Trafalgar Square and a charge will apply. All organisers are required to have Public Liability Insurance to the cover value of £5million. For further information on how to make an application to use the Square please visit our website at london.gov.uk and use the search phrase 'Trafalgar square'.

In response to your request for entertainments licenses, this must be sought from the appropriate local authority. I have included a list of the central London local authorities for you at the end of this letter.

I hope that this information proves useful. Please send my best wishes to Mr Tongue with his performances in London.

Yours sincerely

Lorraine Eyers
Public Liaison Officer

148 Montpelier Rd,
Brighton,
East Sussex,
BN1 2LQ.

The Council of the Isles of Scilly,
Town Hall,
St Mary's,
Isles of Scilly,
TR21 0LW

Dear Sir or Madam,

I am writing to you as the chairman of the 'Gentle Breeze Initiative' based here in Brighton, Sussex. We are at present looking for suitable places for us to take a winter break some time during early December 2004, and the Scilly Islands have been suggested.

Could you forward any material you may have regarding hotel or hostel accommodation, along with some further information with regards to getting to and from Scilly?

As the name of our society indicates, we like to journey to places where we can experience gentle breezes. Travels in the past have taken us as far afield as Laos and Tanzania, but this year we feel we should go for a more 'home-grown' breeze.

Where would be the best place on the Scilly Islands to experience gentle breezes? Presumably some places are going to be better than others? By 'gentle breeze' we mean an extremely light wind that can, at most, ruffle a loose fringe of hair. Anything more than this would be inappropriate for any of our society members, a number of whom are over 75 and susceptible to chills, etc.

If you could get back to me with the information requested I would be most grateful.

Yours truly,

Mary Waters.

COUNCIL of the
ISLES OF SCILLY

TOWN HALL
ST. MARY'S
ISLES OF SCILLY
TR21 0LW
Telephone: (01720) 4225
Fax: (01720) 422202

CLERK, CHIEF EXECUTIVE AND SECRETARY FOR EDUCATION:
P.S. HYGATE, B.A., F.R.S.A.

Phone: 01720 423371
Fax: 01720 423782

This matter is being dealt with by ... **Steve Watt B.Ed Tourism, Development & Maritime Officer** No. ....
E-mail: swatt@scilly.gov.uk

30 July 2004

Mary Waters
148 Montpelier Road
Brighton
East Sussex
BN1 2LQ

Dear Mrs. Waters,

Many thanks for your enquiry about using the Isles of Scilly as a destination for your intriguingly named "Gentle Breeze Initiative."

The choice of destination would be perfect during the summer months during the summer months. Today for instance, we have a very gentle breeze from the North that is just right for cooling the air in this glorious sunshine.

December however, is usually very different. Geographically, as you probably know, we are very exposed and subject to an oceanic climate. Consequently, gentle breeze days are few and far between at that time of year, but that is not to say that we do not get some days of stillness and crystal clear visibility.

Realistically, it might be more appropriate for storm watchers through the winter. I am well acquainted with the wind statistics for I am a very keen windsurfer and look forward to every day when the wind is greater than force 4.

I have sent you a brochure however, and you might wish to consider a different time of year than the winter.

All the best,

Yours sincerely,

Steve Watt

Tourism, Development and Maritime Officer

Packers Unusual Sports Club

148 Montpelier Road, Brighton, East Sussex, United Kingdom, BN1 2LQ.

Glyn-Coch Farm,
St Clears,
Carmarthen,
SA33 4AR

Dear Sir or Madam,

I am writing to you as chairman of the 'Packers Unusual Sports Club' based here in Brighton, Sussex. At present we are working on our itinerary for 2004 and we think we have come up with a quite exceptional piece of field entertainment.

What we have in mind is to hire a number of wolves from a local zoo for the day. We would beforehand have already taken the vital statistics of the aforementioned wolves and had special sheep costumes made up for each particular wolf. These costumes would be made of lightweight lycra with a real sheepskin stitched onto the outside. Professionals assure me that these suits can be made to look very convincing.

We would then come to your farm where you would already have a small flock of sheep stationed in a medium-sized field. We would then let the first costumed wolf into the field. Our members would then take bets as to whether the wolf could get in amongst the pack without the sheep noticing that there was an imposter in their midst. With suitable time intervals the other wolves would be introduced to the field and subsequent bets placed on their projected performance.

Of course, all the wolves would be muzzled before being clothed in their costumes so there would be no danger to your livestock whatsoever.

We really think that this could be an exciting event and one which all the family could enjoy. We can assure you that advanced ticket sales alone could amount to several hundred pounds and we would, of course, be willing to pay a not insubstantial sum for the use of your field and your sheep.

If you could get in touch with me as to the suitability of this event I would be most grateful.

Yours truly,

Derick Pringle.

Glyn-Coch Studios

Crafts, Teas, Woodland Walk,
Camp Site, Artist's Studio

Proprietors: Huw and Thelma Jones

To: -
Mr Derick Pringle
Packers Unusual Sports Club
148, Montpelier Road
Brighton
East Sussex
BN1 2LQ

Glyn-Coch Studios
Ffynnongain Lane, Pwll Trap, St Clears,
Carmarthen SA33 4AR

Tel.   01994 231 867
Fax.   01994 231 863
E-mail   huwandthelma@compuserve.com
Website   www.glyn-coch.com

Thursday, 29 July 2004

Dear Mr Pringle,

Thank you very much for your interesting letter.

However, I am not quite sure whether you are serious or not.

I can understand that someone who had never had any experience with farm animals might think that a visual disguise may be effective. However I can assure you that a disguise such as you proposes would not fool a sheep for a second. The physical posture, the behaviour and the smell of the wolf would all give the game away long before the animal could have said to have 'penetrated' the flock. The introduction of a second wolf would have produced strong pack hunting, driving behaviour among the wolves. The wolves would be separate from and outside the flock.

The above behaviour of the two species means that any gambling would be invalid.

Far more important then the above is the incredible cruelty involved. On detecting the predator the sheep would bunch tightly together and the flock would rotate with risk of injury to weaker sheep. When the predator made its attack, the flock would scatter and try to make its escape charging or trying to jump fences with further risk of injury. The physiological stress may cause heart attacks, and if the exercise was carried out over winter (as appears to be the case as you are still setting up your 2004 programme) miscarriages would be inevitable.

Wolves, like other dogs, do not sweat and control their temperature by panting. Making them wear a heavy insulating sheepskin, would cause them to overheat. This would certainly be the case when zoo animals were suddenly offered the excitement of live prey in this way.

I cannot see any responsible shepherd or zookeeper allowing you to use their animals in this way.

Because your proposal indicates such ignorance, and that there is a possibility of an innocent explanation I will give you the benefit of the doubt and allow you 7 days to reply, and explain what you are really trying to do. If I have not heard from you by Thursday 5th August I will forward your letter to DEFRA, the RSPCA and Sussex Police.

Yours truly,

Huw Jones

Packers Unusual Sports Club

148 Montpelier Road, Brighton, East Sussex, United Kingdom, BN1 2LQ.

25.09.04

Steve & Della Jones,
Grippfinn Finnsheep Stud,
RMB 4518,
Morwell 3840,
Australia.

Dear Sir or Madam,

I am writing to you as chairman of the 'Packers Unusual Sports Club' based here in
Brighton, United Kingdom. At present we are working on our itinerary for 2005 and we
think we have come up with a quite exceptional piece of field entertainment.

What we have in mind is to hire a number of sheep for the day. We would beforehand
have already taken the vital statistics of the aforementioned sheep and had special wolf
costumes made up for each particular sheep. These costumes would be made of
lightweight lycra with a simulated wolfskin stitched onto the outside. Professionals assure
me that these suits can be made to look very convincing.

We would then come to your farm where you would already have a small flock of sheep
stationed in a medium-sized field. We would then let the first costumed sheep in wolf's
clothing into the field. Our members would then take bets as to whether the sheep in
wolf's clothing could get in amongst the pack without the sheep noticing that there was
an imposter in their midst. With suitable time intervals the other sheep in wolf's clothing
would be introduced to the field and subsequent bets placed on their projected
performance.

We really think that this could be an exciting event and one which all the family could
enjoy. We can assure you that advanced ticket sales alone could amount to several
thousand dollars and we would, of course, be willing to pay a not insubstantial sum for
the use of your field and your sheep.

If you could get in touch with me as to the suitability of this event I would be most
grateful.

Yours truly,

Derick Pringle.

GIPPFINN
FINN - FRIESIAN STUD
Steve & Della Jones
www.finnsheep.com
gippfinn@net-tech.com.au

RMB 4518
Morwell 3840
0351223328
0427041253

7 October 2004

Packers Unusual Sports Club,
Mr Derick Pringle,
Dear Sir,

We would be delighted to host your fascinating event. It gladdens the heart to have such a delightful invitation. Too much in life is too serious.

What time of year did you have in mind? There are times which are more awkward than others eg lambing (July) but we always have other sheep which could be used (maiden ewes, rams etc) and fields which are not full of lambing ewes. How many sheep did you have in mind and how large a field? This is the most verdant part of Australia but is sometimes less appealing to the eye than others (eg late summer). Autumn and spring are of course the most lush. It all looks beautiful right now and we are beginning to cut hay and silage and of course are overflowing with spring lambs. Our bottom farm is all river flats so it is always possible to drive onto it and park. We shear in November so just before Xmas the sheep are naked and it would be easier to put costumes on. At other times of the year the size of the costume would have to take into account the length of the wool. We have no wolves in Australia (just like Britain) but I'm sure the sheep will react interestingly to other sheep in disguise. Even when they are shorn they are for a time unable to recognise each other and carry on in an unusual way. The nature and interest of the betting should be wonderful.

Look forward to hearing from you again soon.

Cheers.

Yours faithfully,

Steve & Della Jones

153

148 Montpelier Rd,
Brighton,
East Sussex,
BN1 2LQ.

Robert Walker
Parks Manager,
Brighton and Hove City Council,
Bartholomew House,
Bartholomew Square,
Brighton,
BN1 1JP

Dear Sir,

I am writing to voice a number of complaints that I have to do with the running and maintenance of your park. I am a pensioner and I have lived in the vicinity of your park for the last 50 years. In fact I have a fine view through one of my windows of your park and this, in fact, leads me to my first area of complaint.

Year upon year there are more and more people to be found lying about on the grass. By and large they are mostly young people who seem to have nothing better to do than read books or sunbathe. I have even seen young couples groping and kissing and I think this sort of behaviour is disgusting, I really do! But more importantly all these so-called people are causing untold contamination of the grasses. There was a time when parks employed 'keep off the grass' signs for this very reason, but I can see that hygiene has now gone out of the window, as it were.

I am reliably informed that a large expanse of grass if kept free of any contact with humans is relatively self-maintaining. But there cannot be one bit of grass in your park that has not been polluted with DNA and other bodily secretions. And I am not even going to step onto the subject of dogs.

Related to my first area of complaint is the little matter of your pond. Alike with grass, water can maintain a certain purity if it is left to its own devices. But in your park I have seen little children paddling in this water! Not only that but they are sharing that contaminated water with dirty creatures such as ducks and geese. Add to this the dirty and slimy fish that I have heard about and you are talking about one horrendous concoction of avian, fish and mammalian bacteria.

I am really not sure what the world is coming to. I should like a reply to my letter stating the park policy that you employ and whether you are at all cognisant of any of my extremely pressing concerns.

Edna Burly.

Brighton & Hove

ENVIRONMENT

Brighton & Hove City Council
Bartholomew House
Bartholomew Square
Brighton BN1 1JP

Ms Edna Burly
148 Montpelier Road
Brighton
BN1 2LQ

Date:	29th July 2004
Our Ref:	
Phone:	(01273) 292219
Fax:	(01273) 292227
e-mail:	robert.walker@brighton-hove.gov.uk

Dear Ms Burly,

Thank you for your letter about health risks in parks.

I do not think that the activities you describe on the grass areas will be contaminating the grass.

If children play in the ponds in the parks it could pose a health risk. We do try to keep children out of all of the freshwater ponds.

We will continue in our attempts to keep people out of the fresh water ponds, but we will not be stopping people from lying on the grass.

Yours sincerely,

Robert Walker
Parks Operations Manager

148 Montpelier Rd,
Brighton,
East Sussex,
United Kingdom,
BN1 2LQ

10.09.04

MTA New York City Transit,
180 Livingstone Street,
Room 635b,
Brooklyn,
NY 11201,
USA

Dear Sir or Madam,

Last week my family and I arrived back at London Heathrow Airport. We were returning from a week's glorious holiday in the Big Apple and excited to be returning for our youngest son's fifth birthday party. Unfortunately the aforementioned festivity was marred by the unwarranted misplacement of our son's pet goldfish 'Slurpy'. We have checked with the New York Cab Company but they have no records of retrieving any pet goldfish. We have therefore come to the conclusion that 'Slurpy' must have been left on the Subway train.

When travelling with 'Slurpy' we normally transport him in a see-through polythene bag, but in this instance, due to unforeseen circumstances, he was transported in a white Walmart carrier bag filled with water.

Has one of your employees handed in such a bag to lost property? We realise that they may just have thought it was a bag of water, and not realised that 'Slurpy' was inside at the time.

I recognise that this request may seem a trifle absurd but I can assure you that Timothy is quite distraught with the loss of his pet and I am therefore having to go to great lengths in order to try and ascertain what has happened to his fish.

Could you contact me if you have any pertinent information relating to 'Slurpy's' disappearance.

Yours faithfully,

Guy Piran.

370 Jay Street
Brooklyn, NY 11201

Lawrence G. Reuter
President

 **New York City Transit**

October 14, 2004

Mr. Guy Piran
148 Montpelier Rd.,
Brighton
East Sussex,
United Kingdom
BN12LQ

Dear Mr. Piran,

Please excuse our tardiness in responding to you inquiry.   Since your letter was not sent
to the Lost Property Unit directly, it had to be redirected.

This was such an unusual request that my staff and I all got involved in making inquiries
about the possible sighting of Slurpy's container.   Our hearts are touched by little
Timothy's plight, and it is with sincere regret that I have to inform you that we have had
no reported finding of a white Walmart carrier bag of any kind.

I realize that Slurpy meant the world to Timothy and hope that with such a caring parent,
he will survive his loss.

I am also concerned that my letter may rehash the pain of losing his dear pet.   Please
examine this possibility before mentioning the fact that your quest to retrieve Slurpy, for
him, proved fruitless.

Sincerely,

Eulette Stewart-Graham
Supervisor Lost Property Unit

148 Montpelier Rd,
Brighton,
East Sussex,
BN1 2LQ.

Customer Relations,
First Great Western Trains,
Venture House,
37 Belgrave Street,
Reading,
RG1 1PZ

Dear Sirs,

I am writing to you with regards to a somewhat 'delicate' matter. Last Tuesday I travelled to Reading and unwittingly left a plain brown briefcase on the train. The case was unlocked and I am therefore presuming that the lost property department will by now have viewed the rather unusual contents.

The vintage pornography contained within was to be used for my research purposes as a writer (I am writing a book about 19th Century pornography and the underlying damage it inflicted upon society as a whole). The photographs themselves are incredibly rare and therefore of some considerable value, and I would dearly like to get my hands on them again.

Have you got these items in your possession? If so, I will be more than happy to make a considerable donation to you in order to facilitate their swift return. For personal reasons it would be better if you could reply to this query via letter. I should also be most grateful if you could clearly address any correspondence with my name and mark the top left hand corner of the letter with the written phrase 'Children's Greeting Cards'

Thank you for your time and I hope any reply can be in the affirmative.

Yours sincerely,

Guy Piran

Our Ref: 58084

Great Western Link
Customer Relations
Venture House
37 Blagrave Street
Reading RG1 1PZ

Tel:0845 330 7182
Fax:0118 957 9006

Mr G Piran
148 Montpelier Road
Brighton
BN1 2LQ

29 July 2004

Dear Mr Piran ,

Thank you for your recent communication.

We were sorry to hear of your recent loss of some property and can confirm that we have recorded the report of the loss of your plain brown briefcase on our lost property database.

Regrettably, to date there has been no trace of any such item(s) being handed in either directly to us or to any of the outstations under our control. Should the item(s) belatedly appear then we would naturally arrange for you to be advised as soon as possible.

You say that you travelled to Reading last Tuesday, however as your letter is undated it is difficult to work out exactly which Tuesday you refer. If you could let me know the actual date, also which route you took to reach Reading. I can then begin to work out which lost property office to direct you to if need be. I have spoken to the First Great Western LPO but they have nothing.

If you address your letter to me at the above address I will take care of things from there.

Yours sincerely,

Brian Fearneyhough

Brian Fearneyhough
Customer Relations

First Great Western Link Limited
Registered in England & Wales number 4804687
Milford House, 1 Milford Street, Swindon SN1 1HL

Alexander Literary, Film and Television Agency

148 Montpelier Road, Brighton, East Sussex, United Kingdom, BN1 2LQ.

Carradog House Job Centre,
Cardiff,
Wales

Dear Sir or Madam,

I am writing to you as managing director of the Alexander Agency here in Brighton. We are a busy agency specialising in magazine publications. One of our newest publications is a magazine called 'Tramp'. This magazine sells to an exclusive Eastern European market. There is also a minor but enthusiastic interest in Germany and Denmark.

We are looking to hire models for this magazine for photographic shoots in October 2004. We will be paying a flat rate of £100 a day including a wide assortment of refreshments. Ideally we would prefer to hire tramps that look like they have been on the road for a long time, and those that dress in long trenchcoats and actually resemble the archetypal tramp. To this end we are not interested therefore in people who only have a drink problem and dress in more customary clothes.

Although of a somewhat erotic and explicit nature, we would not be expecting models to participate in any penetrative sex. However, they would be expected to participate in quite revealing poses, as that is what our readership buys the magazine for.

Could you write back and tell me if we would be able to advertise with you, and further to this whether you would in fact be able to actively conscript some tramps from your books, as it were?

I look forward to hearing from you soon.

Yours truly,

Guy Piran

Managing Director

Jobcentre Plus
Employer Services Directorate
Level 2, Steel City House, West Street, Sheffield, S1 2GQ

www.jobcentreplus.gov.uk

Mr. Guy Piran
Alexander Literary, Film and Television Agency
148 Montpelier Road
Brighton
East Sussex
BN1 2LQ

06 August 2004

Dear Mr Piran,

Thank you for your recent letter regarding recruitment. It has been passed to me to provide a response, as I am responsible for Jobcentre Plus employer policy.

It is Jobcentre Plus policy to accept vacancies across a wide range of occupations, on the understanding that they are fully compliant with UK employment legislation and civil law. We therefore require all employers, using Jobcentre Plus services to provide:

- A full and clear Job Description (which is lawful and unambiguous to our customers);
- A rate of pay equal to, or more than that stated in the National Minimum Wage Act;
- A guarantee that all other terms and conditions of employment are lawful; and
- An assurance that all jobs are available on an open and fair basis to jobseeking customers using our services.

In addition however, as an employment agency/business our conditions of acceptance would require you to:

- Complete and return a Service Level Agreement used for agencies to advertise vacancies with us; and
- Complete and return a National Minimum Wage Assurance Stencil.

As long as you are willing to conduct your business on this basis, we can accept your vacancies and will refer appropriate customers interested in employment with you. To notify details please call Employer Direct on 0845 601 2001.

Finally, since receiving your original request about Models, (addressed to Carradog House Jobcentre, Cardiff), I have received a second letter for Street Performers (addressed to Stratford Jobcentre). Without the necessary assurances detailed above, Jobcentre Plus is unable to consider either of these opportunities or any others.

Yours sincerely

Sandy Davidson
Head of Employer Business Support

161

Alexander Literary, Film and Television Agency

148 Montpelier Road, Brighton, East Sussex, United Kingdom, BN1 2LQ.

The Manager,
Downhill House Hotel,
Ballina,
County Mayo,
Ireland

Dear Sir or Madam,

My agency has recently been approached by the 'We Believe in Leprechauns Society' in order for us to help facilitate the accommodation requirements for a week's stay in Ireland for a number of its members. They are wishing to stay off-season for the week commencing 20/11/04. They would be hoping to hire the entire hotel for this period and are willing to pay additional funds to you in lieu of this inconvenience. They would also be happy to pay above the going rate for full-board accommodation.

As a leading company involved in corporate entertainment and hospitality we would also like to suggest an additional feature that you may be able to provide which, we think, would greatly enhance their stay. Are there any local people in you locale with the required physical statistics that would enable them to dress up as leprechauns and look realistic and convincing? We would have to exclude the obvious first choice of children for a number of reasons, not least the friendly yet ribald nature of the society members after they've imbibed sufficient quantities of Guinness. If you do have any adults in mind our agency would be more than happy to pay actors rates on a daily basis for their willing participation. Our agency can provide props such as golden pots filled with replica gold coins, not to mention any number of limericks and rhyming couplets with which they could converse with the 'We Believe in Leprechauns Society' members.

I should be most grateful if you could reply as soon as possible, so that my agency can make all the requisite arrangements.

Yours sincerely,

Guy Piran.

Managing Director

Downhill House Hotel Limited

Our ref/KD

29th July 2004

Mr Guy Piran
Managing Director
Alexander Literary, Film and Television Agency
148 Montpelier Road
Brighton
East Sussex BNI 2LQ
England

Dear Mr Piran

Thank you for your letter received this morning. I have pleasure in enclosing our current brochure, together with tariff, Downhill House Hotel Newsletter and rates for your perusal.

I talked with the local Theatre Co and they have given me the name of a selection of actors Agencies with telephone numbers you can make contact with. The names as follows

The Agency   01 6618535
Phil Stafford   01 2985944
TNE Enrerprises   01 2887537

At the moment we would have 55 rooms available from 20th November for one week - this changes on a daily basis.

Guests staying with us have the complete use of Eagles health & Leisure Club at the hotel with its two swimmingpools, steamroom, sauna, jaccuzzi, sunbed, fully equipped gym with qualified staff and three all weather floodlit tennis courts.

You can view the property by visiting our website at www.downhillhotel.ie .

Should you decide to stay with us you are assured a warm welcome and a very enjoyable stay.

Yours sincerely

Kay Devine

Kay Devine
Marketing manager

BALLINA, CO. MAYO, IRELAND.   Tel: + 353 96 21033   Fax: + 353 96 21338
Email: info@downhillhotel.ie   www.downhillhotel.ie
Managing Director: Mrs Ann Moylett

148 Montpelier Rd,
Brighton,
East Sussex,
BN1 2LQ.

IA International Artistes,
Lapley Hall,
Lapley,
Staffordshire,
ST19 9JR

Dear Sir or Madam,

I am writing to you as the club chairman of the East Sussex Seven-a-Side Rugby Club. In celebration of our club's tenth anniversary we are holding a weekend long carnival at our club grounds on the outskirts of Brighton. The provisional weekend will be the first Sat/Sun in September. As part of this extravaganza we are holding a number of charity matches, and it is with one of these in mind that I am contacting you in this instance.

Would it be possible for your agency to provide two sets of seven dwarves and two Snow Whites? We can provide all the necessary sports clothing and shoes for the dwarves and both Snow Whites, and they would then be expected to play a ten-minutes each way match of rugby, as training will be given on the day. In any case, any such match will clearly not be taken seriously and will be just good, clean knockabout fun.

In addition would any of your dwarves be amenable to being thrown. We can easily provide Velcro suits and a suitable landing board. Dwarves being thrown would obviously be paid in addition for these services.

I should also point out that any Snow Whites that you have in mind should be well aware beforehand of the sometimes excitable nature of our rugby players. To this end we would recommend that you choose Snow Whites less for their golden thigh-length trestles and more for their brawn. By the time our members have drunk fifteen pints they'd find a 300lb Gloucester pig attractive!

I hope you can write back in the affirmative as we would like to make all the requisite arrangements as soon as possible.

Yours truly,

Guy Phran

IA

INTERNATIONAL ARTISTES

Guy Piran
148 Montpelier Road
Brighton
East Sussex
BN1 2LQ

30th July 2004

Dear Mr Piran,

Thank you for your enquiry regarding the possibility of engaging some dwarves and 'Snow Whites' for your event in September.

We would be able to provide the following:

14 dwarves @ £500 each	=	£7000
2 Snow Whites @ £500 each	=	£1000
Total		<u>£8000</u>

If you would like to progress with the idea, please let me know. I can be reached on the number below.

Kind regards

Chris Davis

Midlands office: Lapley Hall, Lapley, STAFFORDSHIRE, ST19 9JR
Telephone: +44 (0)1785 841 991   Fax: +44 (0)1785 841 992

Head office: 4th Floor, Holborn Hall, 193 - 197 High Holborn, LONDON, WC1V 7BD
Telephone +44 (0)20 7025 0600   Fax +44 (0)20 7404 9865
Website www.intart.co.uk   Email (name)@intart.co.uk

REGISTERED IN ENGLAND No. 1957239. LION HOUSE, RED LION STREET, LONDON WC1R 4GB.
MEMBERS OF THE PERSONAL MANAGERS ASSOCIATION & ENTERTAINMENT AGENTS ASSOCIATION LTD.

Alexander Literary, Film and Television Agency

148 Montpelier Road, Brighton, East Sussex, United Kingdom, BN1 2LQ.

Richard Branson,
Virgin Management Ltd,
120 Campden Hill Rd,
London,
W8 7AR

Dear Richard,

I am writing to you as the Managing Director of the 'Alexander Literacy, Film and Television Agency' based here in the UK. One of my clients, Harry Addersley, has recently completed the quite extraordinary feat of crawling east to west across the entire state of Texas. He will be writing a book this fall about his adventures in Texas and I will be marketing the book next year to tie in with his commencement of an altogether more mammoth undertaking: Harry will be attempting to crawl right round the world.

He envisages that it will probably take him anywhere between 12 and 15 years to complete this enormous task but his mind is set on it and he will be hoping to keep a journal of his adventure which our agency will market along with his first book.

The reason I am writing to you is because my client is looking for corporate sponsorship for his record-breaking crawl. The sponsorship money will more often than not go towards the cost of cushion support pads for his knees and hands. He envisages getting through quite a few of these in the course of his journey.

Would you be interested in helping to fund this most remarkable feat? We considered that because you are well acquainted with round-the-world record attempts you might be more sympathetic to what my client has in mind. My client would also be more than willing to wear any 'Virgin' insignia in exchange for any sponsorship deal.

If you could get back in touch with me to tell me of your decision I would be most grateful.

Yours truly,

Guy Piran.

(Managing Director).

Our Ref: dg/030804/1fj

3rd August 2004

Guy Piran
Alexander Literary, FIlm & Television Agency
148 Montpelier Road
East Sussex BN1 2LQ

Dear Guy

Many thanks for your letter and sponsorship proposal.

We all loved your project but simply cannot become corporate sponsors as we have already spent our budget for the next two years and are unable to commit to anything else for the time being.

I'm sorry I have to let you down but I wish you the best of luck.

Kind regards

Richard Branson
Chairman
Virgin Group of Companies

(Dictated by Richard Branson and signed in his absence)

Alexander Literary, Film and Television Agency

148 Montpelier Road, Brighton, East Sussex, United Kingdom, BN1 2LQ.

Ref: nutwriter443x

13.09.04

Air Canada Customer Solutions,
PO Box 64239,
5512-4th Street, NW
Calgary, AB, Canada T2K 6J0

Dear Sir or Madam,

I am at present the literary agent representing the writer Richard Flemming. Richard is hoping to travel by air in the near future, and we would like to find an airline that will accommodate him and his 'friend'. His 'friend' is a garden gnome called Platypus who is three feet high and made out of plaster.

When I first met Richard he was clearly aware that Platypus was a figurative and yet inanimate object. I am sorry to say that that is not now the case, and he presently believes that Platypus is very much a real person. Not only this, but he believes that his 'friend' is the only 'person' he can trust in the publishing business. This has especially upset his publisher, who now has to convince Platypus of the need of changes to manuscripts, book covers, itineraries, etc. I am not best pleased myself to have to conduct ridiculous conversations with a brightly coloured garden gnome, but I continue to represent Richard because he is an accomplished and best-selling author.

I mention the above in detail because we would like any airline to be well aware of Richard's peccadillos right from the start. In this way we hope that no unintentional offence could occur to Richard or, indeed, to your hostess staff.

Platypus will be requiring a window seat next to Richard in the no smoking section. He will have to be addressed in all seriousness as any other passenger (for example, he will undoubtedly have to have his seatbelt fastened by a steward). He will also need to be served food along with Richard. On occasions where a personal preference is required Richard will undoubtedly answer for his 'friend'. However, he will do this as if he is a ventriloquist and therefore he will not be expecting to draw attention to himself. Sadly, he is a far better writer then he is a ventriloquist, so it is sometimes hard to act in a convincingly complicit manner.

Platypus will undoubtedly wish to travel to the lavatory at least once during the flight and we would ask that seating arrangements be made for Richard and his friend that minimise his contact with other passengers who will obviously be unaware of Richard's rather unusual relationship.

I hope you can get back in touch with me with any other questions you may have regarding our requests and as to whether you can accommodate Richard Flemming and Platypus.

Yours truly,

Guy Piran.

AIR CANADA 🍁

Air Canada Customer Solutions
PO Box 64239
5512-4th Street, NW
Calgary, AB, Canada T2K 6J0
Fax 1-866-584-0380 (403) 569-5333

September 28 2004

Reference: 366816

Mr. Guy Piran
Alexander Literary, Film and Television Agency
148 Montpelier Road
Brighton, East Sussex
BN1 2LQ
UK

Dear Mr. Piran:

Thank you for your letter of September 13, 2004.

Without judging Mr. Flemming's condition, we wish to advise you that for both safety and security reasons, we cannot comply with your request.

We trust you can understand that if there is an emergency evacuation or potential decompression, our Flight Attendants must be able to communicate directly to our passengers, and not through another party.

We regret we may have disappointed you, Mr. Piran, however, we do thank you for considering Air Canada.

Sincerely,

Debbie McC

Debbie McAmmond
Customer Solutions

148 Montpelier Rd,
Brighton,
East Sussex,
BN1 2LQ.

Ibstock Brick Ltd,
Ibstock,
Leicestershire,
LE67 6HS

Dear Sir or Madam,

I am writing to you with what I know will seem like a very unusual request. My husband, Denis, died in April of this year and was duly cremated. He worked for over forty years in the building trade, and in his latter years he ran his own highly successful building company. His last will and testament, however, has left my family in something of a quandary. Most of us would have liked for his ashes to be sprinkled on his favourite spot of the beach here in Brighton, but his own stipulation was that he would like for any such remains to be sprinkled, during the manufacturing process, into your own brand bricks. I know that he always remained loyal to certain brands of building materials, and also that for the last ten years or so he used only your bricks whenever he was involved in any of his numerous erections.

It is with some reluctance that my family has now agreed that we should try and honour his last wishes, and that is why I am writing to you now. Would it be possible to have his remains transported to your factory and included in the manufacture of a new consignment of bricks? I guess what my husband thought was that even in death he could act as a firm and reliable foundation for a new family and their evolving lives. Perhaps there is a certain poetry in this.

If you are amenable to this request we can have his ashes transported to your manufacturing works. With a little discretion, very few people would need to know what was afoot, and certainly no one at the building end of things will have even the slightest knowledge of any unusual event having taken place.

I should be most grateful if you could get back to me as to whether you can accede to such a request. If not, then I guess we will just have to try some of the competitive brands as a last resort.

Yours truly,

Mavis Bunson.

IBSTOCK ™
innovators in clay

Our Ref: KM/757/jm
4 August 2004

Mrs M Bunson
148 Montpelier Road
Brighton
East Sussex
BN1 2LQ

Dear Mrs Bunson

Your letter addressed to Ibstock Brick's Dorket Head factory has been referred to me for attention.

Can I offer my condolences on the loss of your husband in April this year and reassure you that we, at Ibstock Brick Limited are ready to help you in connection with your husband's stipulation, as outlined in your letter.

You are right to say that it is, indeed, an unusual request, and I believe equally right to find the poetic nature of your husband's request to 'live on', as it were, through his chosen route.

We brickmakers rely on the skills and experience of many people in the construction of our built environment, so perhaps it is appropriate that a lifelong member of the building trade would seek to find immortality by this route?

Whilst your letter was addressed to our factory in Nottingham, we do in fact operate 24 factories in the UK, a number of which are much closer to your home. It may be that a location nearer to Brighton would be more appropriate? If, of course, Nottingham is important to you, then that is fine.

In light of the importance of the way in which you would like your husband's request to be carried out, I think it would probably help if I was to come and meet you (and / or your family) at a convenient time. We could then discuss your wishes, and perhaps I can advise on practical issues at the factory and help you to understand what may be possible or appropriate.

IBSTOCK ™
innovators in clay

Cont'd...

We would need to involve only a small number of people at the factory; and rest assured we can deal with this both sensitively and with discretion.

Is it possible to speak to you, or a member of your family, over the telephone? If so, I would appreciate a contact telephone number. This would help in making arrangements etc.

A number of questions present themselves, such as, do you have a special date (or day) in mind? and do you know which brand or name of brick your husband most preferred to build with?

May I ask you please to suggest to me a choice of possible dates on which we could meet? I am away on holiday as from 5th August, returning to work on 19th August. In the meantime, your contact at Ibstock would be my secretary, Judy Mugleston. Judy's telephone number is 01530 257247 and she is based at our Ibstock Office at the address below.

Finally, rest assured that we will try to help, as you say in your letter, to honour your husband's last wishes.

Yours sincerely

Keith Morton

Keith Morton
Production Director

Alexander Literary, Film and Television Agency

148 Montpelier Road, Brighton, East Sussex, United Kingdom, BN1 2LQ.

Ref: 77yrt54

Bruce Commercial Estate Agents,
94 Upper Walkway,
West Yard,
Camden Lock,
London,
NW1 8AF

Dear Sir or Madam,

My colleagues and I are writing to you, as we are interested in renting one of your offices on a leasehold basis. We would be negotiating the hire of the office space on behalf of a client company of ours – the Nightmare Re-enactment Co-operative. We have represented this co-operative for a number of years now and have negotiated both previous leaseholds.

The Nightmare Re-enactment Co-operative is an arts-based and government funded body which comprises a number of different professionals drawn from a wide range of therapeutic communities. The body was established in 1993 to work primarily with people in the community that suffer from severe sleep deprivation due to recurrent nightmares. The co-operative also works with other sleeping anxiety disorders.

Working on a very pragmatic level the co-operative uses its own office space to stage re-enactments of an individual person's nightmares. That is why large open-plan spaces are vital to the organisers, as this gives them the largest amount of scope to create realistic and convincing nightmare vistas – ones which they hope, for the sufferer, will have a convincing verisimilitude.

The aim of the therapy is to walk people through their nightmares and anxiety dreams and actually be there in person as the nightmare occurs. This usually gives the sufferer a certain reassurance that they have never experienced before, and after a number of sessions they are often quite happy to finally go it alone without any assistance. Many of these 'cured' sufferers actually find themselves laughing right the way through the nightmare in the end, wondering how they could have been so scared of lions, tigers, devils, falling, etc, in the first place.

For a few, however, getting to this laughter stage is impossible. With these particular people in mind the therapists, over a number of sessions, walk the sufferer through his nightmare and then into a newly created happy ending scenario. Among the therapists this is affectionately known as 'Enid-Blightoning'. The success rate, avoiding recidivism, for this second type of sufferer is still of a magnitude to make it worthwhile.

My clients would wish to be importing into your office space large quantities of sophisticated film and video equipment, lighting, and stage props and scenery. Along with this they would also be wishing to create clear and safe storage facilities for any animals that might be required. I should add that any animals brought in would be there for the day only (we actually have an existent agreement between our clients and London Zoo that stipulates return of animals on a same day basis).

Do you think you may be able to accommodate my clients? I am presuming that you may have a number of other questions that you may like to put to us, so please do not hesitate to contact my agency with any other queries.

Yours truly,

Guy Piran.

r G Piran
exander Literary Film & Television Agency
48 Montpelier Road
righton
AST SUSSEX
3N1 2LQ

Bruce

COMMERCIAL ESTATE AGENTS
TEL +44 (0) 20 7267 6772
FAX +44 (0) 20 7267 0660

LKB/CD

29th July 2004

Dear Mr Piran

RE: OFFICE SPACE

Please find enclosed our latest list for your information and would draw your attention to our website which has all of our properties, with pictures and is totally up to date.

If you wish to view any of these properties, please call us in the office so we can arrange viewings and if you have an email address, please forward it to us so we can place you on our mailing list.

Yours sincerely

Christine Dowsett

Enc

148 Montpelier Rd,
Brighton,
East Sussex,
BN1 2LQ.

Newhaven Cemetery,
Lewes Rd,
Newhaven,
East Sussex

Dear Sir or Madam,

My husband was killed last week in a tragic boating accident in Hawaii. We are awaiting the American coroner's inquest to his death and hope to have his remains flown back to the United Kingdom as soon as possible. My family and I would dearly like for Terry to be buried in the Woodvale Cemetery, as it is where he spent many happy hours walking with our pet dogs.

Terry was a very enthusiastic collector of children's toys and more importantly was the head of the East Sussex Lego Society. He dedicated much of his spare time to running this society and organising charity Lego-building events. He will be greatly missed by one and all. Indeed, one of the directors of the aforementioned society has suggested to my family that it would be highly appropriate, considering Terry's commitment to Lego in general, to have any memorial built out of Lego bricks as opposed to the customary stone or marble.

My family and I consider this to be a charming idea. Not only would it stand as a significant and truly relevant memorial to one man's lifelong commitment, but all of those people who shared his enthusiasm would be able to take an active part in building his memorial themselves.

To this end would it be possible to build an old-fashioned sarcophagus-like memorial? As opposed to the customary technique of Lego building, all the many thousands of bricks would be finally superglued into place. When complete we envisage it would have the structural strength of any granite erection and because of its plastic nature, a great deal more longevity.

I hope you can get back in touch with me soon to tell us whether you can accommodate our wishes.

Yours truly,

Mrs Dinah Clarke.

NEWHAVEN TOWN COUNCIL

IAN EVEREST
TOWN CLERK

TOWN COUNCIL OFFICES
18 FORT ROAD
NEWHAVEN
EAST SUSSEX
BN9 9QE

Mrs D Clarke
148 Montpelier Road
BRIGHTON
East Sussex
<u>BN1 2LQ</u>

Tel: (01273) 516100
Fax: (01273) 611175
Email: newhaventc@mistral.co.uk

Your Ref.:
Our Ref.:   IE/sb

3rd August 2004

Dear Mrs Clarke,

<u>NEWHAVEN CEMETERY</u>
<u>LEWES ROAD, NEWHAVEN</u>

Thank you for your recent letter containing details of your husband's tragic death.

Concerning your enquiry about the installation of a Lego-brick memorial, an extract of the rules and regulations of Newhaven Cemetery state that "no memorial shall be erected which is constructed of wood or of bath, caen, soft or artificial stone of any description or of any manufactured material, except that a temporary wooden cross may be installed for a period not exceeding 3 months. Memorials shall be constructed of granite, marble, slate or other hard natural stone of monumental quality ....".

I am sorry to have to say, therefore, that a memorial of the type you describe would not be permitted.

Please accept my condolences on your sad loss.

Yours sincerely,

Ian Everest
Town Clerk

148 Montpelier Rd,
Brighton,
East Sussex,
BN1 2LQ.

Heinz Consumer Feedback,
South Building,
Hayes Park,
Hayes,
Middlesex,
UB4 8AL

To whomsoever it may concern,

It's disgusting, that's what it is! Disgusting! Disgusting! Disgusting! I could carry on saying disgusting for a very long time and it still wouldn't explain how disgusted I am. I mean, the soup's alright- it's got quite a nice flavour really. But all the other stuff. It makes me want to puke.

And what about all the children? Did you ever think about them? What are they going to grow up thinking? That this is the way life is? That it's quite acceptable for them to do this and that because the 'big boys' like you do it?

And I'm not even going to get on to the subject of experimentation. Suffice it to say that there are people all over the place that do not have their heads in the sands. You can fool some of the people all of the time but you can't fool all of the people some of the time. Someone famous once said that, and they weren't wrong. I'm not famous, I'm just your average urban dweller. That's why you think you can put one over on me. Well, this lady's not for sinking - the drowned rats have departed but I will float on.

I had thought of taking the matter up with the Prime Minister himself, but I bet he's part of the whole thing anyway. Then I thought of the Queen. I'm sure she's wealthy enough not to be directly involved, but she doesn't really have the power anymore (it's a good job we're not living in the Elizabethan Age - you'd end up having all your heads chopped off!). In the end I have decided to let you try to explain yourself first, and if that's not satisfactory then I'm going to go to a secret organisation that you don't know about. They'll be able to take care of everything, no doubt about it.

I await your reply with great interest.

Yours truly,

Eunice McCloud.

H. J. Heinz Company Limited

South Building
Hayes Park
Hayes
Middlesex UB4 8AL
England

Tel: +44(0) 20-8573-7757
Fax: +44(0) 20-8848-2325
www.heinz.co.uk

000890404B

26 August 2004

Ms E Mcloud
148 Montpelier Road
BRIGHTON
BN1 2LQ

Dear Ms Mcloud

Thank you for your recent letter.

I would be grateful if you could contact me on 01942624464 to discuss the matter further.

Thanking you for co-operation in this matter.

Yours sincerely

Geoff Kearsley
Consumer Care Co-ordinator

Alexander Literary, Film and Television Agency

148 Montpelier Road, Brighton, East Sussex, United Kingdom, BN1 2LQ.

Alan Griffiths,
City Parks at Stanmer,
Stanmer Park,
Lewes Rd,
BN1 9SE

Dear Alan,

I am writing to you as the managing director of the Alexander Agency based here in Brighton. We represent clients from the full spectrum of the arts and entertainment, and it is with one client in mind that I am writing to you now.

Heinrich Fuller is a renowned conceptual artist in his native Germany, and in recent years has gained an enormous amount of credibility throughout the rest of the World. He specialises in live body sculpture, requiring complete nudity. Perhaps, you will have seen some of his 'installations' on the television or reported in the national press.

Heinrich has recently moved to Brighton and is currently working on a number of projects. One of his first English works is to be called 'Frictional Intensity' and requires a large area of outside space. We were hoping that we might be able to gain permission from yourselves to make use of a large area of grassland in Stanmer Park.

What Heinrich has in mind is to have 200 naked people of all ages, creeds and nationalities lined up on the grass. They would all be naked, of course, and all of them would be facing the south (passing motorists would only see bare bottoms). Then over the course of an afternoon Heinrich will 'body-rub' himself against each of these individuals in turn. This 'body-rubbing' requires both bottom-to-bottom and front-to-front rubbings and will on average take three minutes per person. Heinrich requires some flexibility in this as, on occasion, he can develop a certain 'magnetism' with a fellow performer. However, these instances are rare and will never go over, say, a ten-minute boundary. Counter to this, there are certainly going to be individuals who he will literally very briefly front-and-bottom rub before hastily moving on up the line. Overall the whole extravaganza should take no more than ten hours.

After the event all the performers will suitably clothe themselves and disperse in an orderly manner .

I have told Heinrich that Brighton is a cosmopolitan and forward-looking town that may well grant him the permission he seeks. I should also take this opportunity to tell you that a number of stewards would be on hand throughout the day to ensure that passers by and the general public do not get in any way 'carried away'. I can assure you that this event will be properly policed.

If you could get back to my agency as soon as possible I would be most grateful, as planning for such an event will no doubt take a considerable amount of time. Please enclose any other questions that you may have about this event in your correspondence.

Yours truly,

Guy Piran.

Brighton & Hove

ENVIRONMENT

Quality of Life & Green Spaces
Brighton & Hove City Council
2nd Floor, Bartholomew House
Bartholomew Square
Brighton BN1 1JP

Guy Piran	Date: 2 August 2004
148 Montpelier Road	Our Ref: PF/vg
Brighton	Your Ref:
East Sussex	Phone: (01273) 295033
BN1 2LQ	Fax: (01273) 292360
	e-mail: pat.foster@brighton-hove.gov.uk

Dear Mr. Piran,

Re: Conceptual Art in Stanmer Park/Beach Pebble Counting/Jumping for Jesus

Thank you very much for your letters on the above topics, which have heightened the entertainment level of my summer post bag.

If you want to count the pebbles on the beach, you will be most welcome. The official advice is that you follow the "safe sun" guidance.

Also, jumping up and down on Hove seafront should not cause a problem, so long as you respect the needs of other seafront pedestrians. The volume of the ukulele and/or trumpet playing should be kept low enough to avoid causing noise nuisance.

I would require more detail of the proposed naked conceptual art project. The council generally discourages "skin to skin" contact in Stanmer Park, or indeed, any park, as it tends to offend a significant portion of the general public. On the basis of your description of the event I must advise that it is unlikely to gain approval.

Yours sincerely,

P. Foster.

Pat Foster
Assistant Director
Environment

Alan Titchmarsh,
Artists Index,
Room 502a,
172-178 Victoria Rd,
London,
W3 6UL

Dear Alan,

I am writing to ask your advice on a specific gardening matter, but may I first take this opportunity to congratulate you on your burgeoning career in the literary field. I bet there can't be many gardeners out there that have ever gone on to become best-selling and successful author as well? I think you are a truly renaissance man, and a bit of a polymath to boot!

My problem is with roses. I have tried umpteen times to establish roses in my garden but each time it has been a miserable failure. I am very new to gardening but even I can see that if there are other flowers growing (which there are - planted by the previous owner of the property) then there should be no real problem with my roses. And I always buy the most expensive roses from the florist, so it can't be down to the quality of the product.

My neighbour thinks that because all my attempts have been relentless disasters that I must be making some basic mistake every time, and that is why I am writing to you. When I get back from the florists I always carefully trim the stems and put the flowers straight into water. I never leave them more than an hour or two, and then I take them out into the garden where I will have already prepared six-inch holes for them. I pop them in one by one and then pack the earth around them. Then I give them a good water. They are usually alright for a day or two but then they always die off. It's very frustrating. My neighbour thinks that I should trim the head as well as the stem in order to give the stem the best chance of taking to the soil. It wouldn't have to concentrate on the head so much then. Is this a good idea?

I am hoping that you could write back with a few suggestions. Perhaps roses are very hard to grow and I should stick to something simple like orchids or marigolds. I do hope you can help.

Yours truly,

Sarah Trollope.

From Alan Titchmarsh

Thank you for your letter. I'm afraid I get so
many requests to solve gardening problems
that I just can't answer them all personally,
though I do try to answer as many of
them as possible on television and in print.
I do hope you'll understand.
With all good wishes.

URBAN MIME INITIATIVE

148 Montpelier Road, Brighton, East Sussex, BN1 2LQ.

The Manager,
Zizzi's Restaurant,
South Rd,
Haywards Heath,
East Sussex

Dear Sir or Madam,

I am writing to you as the activities director of the Urban Mime Initiative. We are soon to celebrate our tenth anniversary, and a number of our members have suggested that we make use of your restaurant for the occasion. Might this be possible? There are, at present, 60 members in the troupe and they would all like to be present at the celebratory meal. If this amount falls well short of your usual amount of covers then we would be happy to make up the 'average' shortfall in order to have the restaurant to ourselves. This is very important to us, not least because there are a number of 'alterations' that we would like you to make to your usual restaurant layout.

For a start we would ask that all tables and chairs be removed from the normal dining area. If they cannot be hidden away from sight then neatly stacked along a wall would be sufficient. We would then ask that when our members arrive they be directed to 'non-existent' tables by your waiting staff. We envisage that these 'non-existent' tables will be round in nature and seat a total of five persons. If your staff are at all put off or intimidated by this arrangement, let me assure you that members of the Urban Mime Initiative are extremely good exponents of mime and will quickly adapt to the seating situation, however well or otherwise this is indicated by your staff. We do not expect your staff to be experts at mime whatsoever, just that they keep in the spirit of the occasion and give it a jolly good go.

Once seated we would ask that your staff hand out imaginary menus, and ask our members if they would like drinks. This 'asking' must also, of course, be mimed, as will be taking down the guests menu selections on an imaginary notebook.

As you will have gathered by now, we will not be requiring any 'real' food to be presented to our members during the course of the meal. We would, however, like to stipulate that the meal occasioned be a seven-course dinner with imaginary coffee and liqueur to follow.

Although you may understandably consider laying off your chef for the evening we would also ask that you do not do this. Just knowing that there is a real chef 'preparing' imaginary food in the kitchen will make all our members imaginary food taste all the sweeter.

In terms of payment for your endeavour we would like to suggest paying you a one-off fee proportionate to what your average takings would have normally been on that particular night.

I'm sure you don't receive requests like this every day of the week, but I hope you can give it due and reasonable consideration. Please write back to me with any other concerns or queries that you may have.

Yours truly,

Xavier Lacombe.

BLUE HAWAII RESTAURANT
2 RICHMOND ROAD, KINGSTON, SURREY KT2 5EB
Tel: 020 8549 6989 Fax: 020 8546 1650 www.bluehawaii.co.uk

Mr. Xavier Lacombe
Urban Mime Initiative
148 Montpelier Road
Brighton
East Sussex
BN1 2LQ

Dear Mr. Lacombe

My name is Talib Araim and I am the owner of the Blue Hawaii restaurant in Kingston, Surrey. I came across your details when I was trying to book a meal for my staff in a restaurant called Zizzi's. The date that we had in mind was not possible because I was told that your society had booked the restaurant for that evening. The person on the phone mentioned that the Zizzi's staff are looking forward to this event as it was going to be a very strange experience. When I heard more details about your plans for that evening, I had to say that the gentleman was right, it did sound like a very interesting evening and it would be something that I would very much like to try.

Being a Hawaiian Themed restaurant, our staff are all trained to be a bit more open, expressive, adaptable, outgoing, in short, professional extraverts. An evening of acting would be very entertaining for us, and hopefully for you.

Should you have any future plans for such events and would like to hold it in a Hawaiian setting with staff dressed in Hawaiian outfits, please do not hesitate to contact me and I'm sure we will be able to accommodate all your requirements.

I thank you for taking the time to read this letter and look forward to discussing this with you further in the near future.

Many thanks

Talib Araim
Proprietor

Please use the contact details below

T. 07958 937 493
F. 020 8399 9742
E. talibaraim@aol.com

Registered Office: 22 Marryat Road, London, SW19 5BD
Registration Number: 2646707
Managing Director: Talib Araim

148 Montpelier Rd,
Brighton,
East Sussex,
BN1 2LQ.

Durex,
SSL International Head Office,
Toft Hall,
Knutsford,
WA16 9PD

Dear Durex,

I am extremely excited! I have taken one of your products and done something extraordinary with it. What I have done to your product is going to revolutionise the whole condom industry. I can see an enormous growth in the industry, and if you join forces with me, as it were, we can both be at the head of this growth. I am now going to tell you what I've done: I have created the World's first talking condom.

The idea came to me when I was watching the Teletubbies. Out of nowhere I had a flash of inspiration and the next minute I was rooting around in the kitchen drawer. Half an hour later, with the help of a recording key-ring fob/pedometer, a roll of sticky-backed-plastic and one of your 'Ultra Safe' condoms, I had created my talking condom.

At first it could just say 'testing one two three, testing one two three' but after using a little bit of imagination I soon gave it a vocabulary of phrases you'd be proud of (I even did the odd one in a fake German accent).

My talking condom now has a repertoire of:

"By heck, it's dark in here."
"Whoa baby, careful, it's my first time."
"Oh my God, will you look at that?"
"I can't take anymore."
"My word, this one's tight."
"We all live in a yellow submarine..."

Words recorded on the pedometer speed up and slow down according to walking pace, but I have found it works just as well when it's sellotaped to a condom that is itself strapped to your erect member. If you're going at it slowly it takes a good while to get through the repertoire; if you're going at it hammer and tongs the yellow submarine makes an appearance every few seconds or so.

This said, I haven't tried it with a real person yet (I don't have a girlfriend at present). However, in my simulated tests it works a treat. For these simulated tests I have had to make use of a large teddy bear in order to gain the friction needed of a solid body (I don't think Bobo has quite got over the shock!!!).

I just know that Durex as a company is going to want to come in on this with me. You'd be stupid not to. I'd like you to write back, tell me what you think and then set up a business meeting where we can get down to basics.

I must inform you, however, that you do have competitors out there (Boots, Virgin, Porkinson's) who will no doubt jump at the chance to get their hands on this idea. I must also tell you that a working model has been deposited with my bank as an insurance measure against breach of copyright.

Don't let this golden opportunity pass you by.

Yours truly,

Guy Piran.

SSL International

GROUP RESEARCH AND DEVELOPMENT

205 Science Park
Milton Road
Cambridge CB4 0GZ
United Kingdom
Tel: +44 (0) 1223 423232
Fax: +44 (0) 1223 423310

Guy Piran
148 Montpelier Road
Brighton
East Sussex BN1 2LQ

Our ref: ADŁ04380

25th August 2004

Dear Guy,

Re: Talking Condom

Your letter to "Durex" regarding the idea for a talking condom has been forwarded to me by Michelle Crux to respond to.

I'm sorry to disappoint you but the idea for musical or talking condoms has been around for many years so you can remove your working model from the bank vault and put your pedometer back to its proper use! As for poor Bobo, the less said the better.

A number of musical condom variants are available over the Internet – see attached web pages, and there are also a number of patents relevant to this area. I have attached copies of three US ones.

These products are gimmicks or novelty products and should not be used for contraception or protection against sexually transmitted infections.

Thank you for sharing your idea with us and if you should have any further ideas for condom products, please do not hesitate to let me know.

Regards,

Yours sincerely,

Dr Adrian Łyszkowski
Chief Research Manager, Group IP

Encl: US5163447, US5524638, US6145506
        Web pages: http://www.bigboycondoms.co.uk/condoms/default.php?cPath=10
                         http://makeupartist.com/frames/condoms.htm

SSL International plc
Registered in England No. 388828.
Registered Office:
35 New Bridge Street, London EC4V 6BW

148 Montpelier Rd,
Brighton,
East Sussex,
BN1 2LQ.

John Whittet,
Whittet Books Ltd,
Hill Farm,
Stonham Rd,
Cotton,
Stowmarket,
Suffolk,
IP14 4RQ

Dear John,

I am extremely, extremely excited!!! I have been doing something for a long time now, which has given me a great deal of personal satisfaction. It has not been until recently, however, that I have realized that there are others out there who share my enthusiasm for what I had thought was my own particular, if not peculiar, pursuit.

I like to kiss animals! There, that's got it off my chest. I am not ashamed, you understand, it's just I'm still a little unused to broadcasting my great passion, even though this is only in letter form.

I started out, probably like everybody else, kissing myself in the mirror. This happened first at about the age of five and continued until I kissed my first girlfriend some eighteen years later. As you can imagine all that self-kissing made me quite an expert at what I would call the 'hard' kiss - and I'm sure if you talked to my first girlfriend today she would be able to corroborate this.

Then I met my wife, and although the kissing decreased rapidly towards the time of our divorce, I think even she would maintain that I was a good kisser all along.

It was only long after Samantha had gone that I started experimenting with animals. There was, however, no conscious decision to apply myself in this way - it just kind of happened naturally. One minute Chester would be licking me in the face in appreciation of having had a good walk and a nice Pedigree Chum dinner, the next I'd have his rather slippery front lips up against mine in a 'hard' kiss. Chester didn't seem to mind in the slightest and sometimes we kissed like this for quite some time. On occasions I even used my tongue in what you might call the 'French' manner.

Chester, sadly, is no more, but since his demise I have bought quite a number of different animals to take his place - and these animals range in size from Matthew the chinchilla to Boris the Shetland pony that now lives in my back garden. I have a tender and loving relationship with all these animals, although I have to say some are better kissers than others!

And I don't just draw the line at kissing. I have become extraordinarily dexterous at petting and stroking too. Sometimes I just do partial body-petting, other times I go the whole hog and give them an 'all-over'.

I would like to share my story with other people out there, and that's why I'm writing to you. Would you like me to send you my manuscript? It contains my full life story so far, along with nearly 250 photographs that I have amassed over the years. I even have one photograph taken by my sister, I think, of me aged about 15 kissing myself in the mirror. That's probably the best example I have in my whole collection of a 'hard' kiss. Some of the latest photographs - including those taken with Boris - are more illuminating of my 'soft' kiss, which I do actually prefer these days.

I obviously can't send you the originals, but the photocopies aren't bad. If you want to take this thing further at a later date then I'd make the photographs available to you then.

I do hope you feel, as I do, that there could be a genuine audience for my book out there amongst the animal-loving public, and I very much look forward to hearing from you soon.

Yours truly,

Eric Potter.

Whittet Books Limited

Eric Potter
148 Montpelier Rd
Brighton
E Sussex BN1 2LQ

Hill Farm Stonham Road Cotton
Stowmarket Suffolk IP14 4RQ
TELEPHONE: (01449) 781877
FAX: (01449) 781898
E MAIL: Annabel@whittet.dircon.co.uk

August 18th, 2004

Dear Eric Potter

Thanks for your letter. An intriguing idea! Certainly very high publicity potential, but I am afraid that I cannot see it as a book, and therefore must decline your offer to publish.

Yours sincerely

Annabel Whittet

Directors: A.J. Whittet, J.A. Whittet
The company is registered in England no 816947   Registered office: Hill Farm, Stonham Road, Cotton, Stowmarket, Suffolk IP14 4RQ

East Sussex GodSquad

148 Montpelier Road, Brighton, East Sussex, BN1 2LQ.

Complaints Department,
Berwick Borough Council Offices,
Wallace Green,
Berwick-upon-Tweed,
TD15 1ED

Dear Sir or Madam,

I am writing to you as the chairman of the East Sussex GodSquad. We are a Christian organization that seeks to actively promote the works and teachings of Jesus Christ. We also take a similar proactive stance with regards to Lucifer, seeking to hinder his diabolical works wherever possible.

It is with this latter work in mind that I am writing to you now. It has come to our attention that the Choral Minster Society of Devil Worshippers (also based here in East Sussex) has paid an undisclosed, and yet not inconsiderable, sum to you in order to have your island temporarily, for the weekend, re-named 'Unholy Island'. We also gather that the weekend in question is penciled-in to be Easter Weekend 2005.

How on earth can you square this with your consciences? Do you not realize that this is just how the Devil and his dirty, lascivious minions seek to wrest control of the World from the one true God. Granted you may have thought that the Choral Minster Society of Devil-Worshippers sounded like an almost quaint and unassuming organization incapable of any real acts of gross debauchery and sin. Let me assure you that this is not the case; and I should know - I used to be one of them, before Christ found me in the bathroom one bleak winter's night and turned me on, to the paths of righteousness.

If you are prepared to go ahead with this abomination let me tell you what the consequences will be. Unless we hear back from you confirming that you have cancelled this sick inversion, we will have no choice other than to mobilize the entire GodSquad forces and make our way up to Holy Island/Unholy Island. We will there do battle with whatever contingents of the Choral Minster Society of Devil Worshippers we find there and expel them from the island. We will do this knowing that God is with us and watching over us, and that he will overlook a little 'rough and tumble' on our part, if it amounts to a victory against his ghastly nemesis. Let me therefore assure you that we are prepared to use whatever degree of force is necessary to accomplish our objectives.

I hope that with the above in mind you will carefully consider whether it would be a good idea to go ahead with this name change, and whether the diabolical money on offer is really worth the trouble that would undoubtedly ensue if you decide to go ahead with this unholiness.

I very much look forward to hearing from you soon,

Yours truly,

Pastor Guy Piran.

Council Offices, Wallace Green
Berwick-upon-Tweed TD15 1ED
Telephone:01289 330044
Facsimile 01289 330540

Web Site: http://www.berwickonline.org.uk
DX 67798 Berwick-upon-Tweed

Jane E Pannell
Chief Executive

W.E. Henry MA, LLB, Borough Solicitor
P.J. Newton BA

The Solicitors to
BERWICK-UPON-TWEED BOROUGH COUNCIL

Our Ref: A/22/1WH
Your Ref:
Date: 2nd August 2004

Please ask for: Mr W E Henry
Direct Telephone: 01289 301710
Email: wh@berwick-upon-tweed.gov.uk

Dear Pastor Piran

CHORAL MINISTER SOCIETY OF DEVIL WORSHIPPERS
HOLY ISLAND

Thank you for your letter (undated) received at these offices on 30th July 2004.

The Council have no knowledge of such a proposal and, in any event, would, I believe, have no authority to agree it.

Yours sincerely

Borough Solicitor

Pastor G Piran
East Sussex GodSquad
148 Montpelier Road
Brighton
East Sussex
BN1 2LQ

193

Alexander Literary, Film and Television Agency

148 Montpelier Road, Brighton, East Sussex, United Kingdom, BN1 2LQ.

25.09.04

Park Authorities,
Battersea Park,
Battersea,
London,
SW11 4NJ

Dear Sir or Madam,

I am writing to you as the managing director of the Alexander Literary , Film and Television Agency. In addition to our regular clients we also represent a number of charities and societies. It is with one such society in mind that I am writing to you in this instance.

The Biblical Re-enactment Society stages charitable and fundraising events throughout the year. Drawing upon biblical sources they seek to re-enact certain scenes and events that allegedly occurred in the bible. For example, last year they put on a remarkable show in Dresden, Germany, which was a re-enactment of the Crucifixion of Christ. I was present at this event and I can assure you the attention to detail was quite astounding. One actually felt that one had been transported back two thousand years in time. I actually found it quite an emotional experience, I have to say.

On a more light-hearted note the society have in the past re-enacted the Expulsion of Adam and Eve from the Garden of Eden (Palace of Versailles gardens '89; The Mews, Chipping Sudbury '98), Moses leading his people into the Promised Land (Scunthorpe Municipal Park '95, Whitley Bay Ice Rink 2000), and Christ overturning the tables of the money-changers (Royal Bank of Scotland '97).

What they are seeking to accomplish in the summer of 2005 is a successful re--enactment of Christ Feeding the Five Thousand. With such large numbers of people involved they are hoping to stage this event in Battersea Park. They realise that this is a municipal park and must remain open to the public. In fact the society is more than happy for people to join in the re-enactment itself.

A certain Gary Higgins who is a long-term member of the Biblical Re-enactment Society, and is also an illusionist extraordinaire, will be overseeing the event and playing the role of Christ. He will be attempting to feed the five thousand (possibly more!) with 2 crates of sardines and twenty loaves of bread. If I am any judge of Gary I imagine that he will accomplish this task with the usual aplomb.

Although many society members will be present there will no doubt still be a need to boost numbers, and to this end we will be contacting a number of charities for the homeless. We are hoping that a number of homeless people will come to the park and avail themselves of free food. The society feels that it will then not only be creating an extraordinary piece of outdoor entertainment, but also giving something back to the community as well.

Would you be able to get back to me on the possibility of allowing the Biblical Re-enactment Society to stage this extraordinary event in Battersea Park. I can assure you that the Society will provide a number of stewards who will be responsible for clearing away any mess that could be left behind after the feeding of the five thousand. Further to this they would be happy to place with you a cash bond in terms of assurance that all park facilities are left in tip-top condition.

I look forward to your response.

Yours truly,

Guy Piran.

Wandsworth

Wandsworth Council
Events and Filming Office
Battersea Park
London SW11 4NJ

Please ask for/reply to: Suzz Bell
Telephone: 020 8871 7116
Fax: 020 7223 7919
Email: suzzbell@wandsworth.gov.uk

Our ref:
Your ref:
Date: 5th October 2004

Guy Piran
Alexander Literary, Film and
Television Agency,
148 Montpelier Road,
Brighton,
East Sussex,
United Kingdom
BN1 2LQ

Dear Mr Piran,

Thank you for your letter dated 25th September, which was passed to me today, about holding a biblical re-enactment in Battersea Park. Before we can really look further into this I would really need to find out more about your proposal.

Please would you contact me on the above number or email address, so that we can discuss this further.

Yours sincerely

Suzz Bell
Events Operations Manager

INVESTOR IN PEOPLE   Awarded for excellence

www.wandsworth.gov.uk

Channel Gliding Club,
Waldershare Park,
Dover,
Kent,
CT15 5NH

148 Montpelier Rd,
Brighton,
East Sussex,
BN1 2LQ.

Dear Sir or Madam,

I am writing to you in the hope that you may be able to offer me information relating to flying lessons. Presumably you accommodate those that wish to book up in advance for a number of flying lessons? I should also like to know how many lessons it will take before I become a proficient flyer. Fortunately I do have some experience in flying, and I hope this will stand me in good stead.

The experience that I have amounts to experimentation that I have conducted in my back garden at home. My first fledgling attempts to fly I now look back on as frankly laughable, but they did certainly cement in me the ambition to fly.

I started off just flapping my arms like a bird. Initially I flapped for half and hour in the morning and one hour in the evening. In both theses sessions I would start off flapping like a buzzard or and albatross, but towards the end of the sessions I would be flapping a bit more like a medium-sized bird. For the first few weeks I had little success, although towards the end of some of my sessions I certainly felt something akin to light-headedness.

I then had a good hard look at my situation and realised that I had made a crucial error: fledglings don't learn to fly on the ground, they learn to fly from the nest. There is an obvious height advantage attached to this method.

I therefore invested in a 6ft stepladder, which aided me considerably in my attempts to fly. Starting off on the lower rungs of the ladder, I gradually made my way further and further up the ladder until I could take-off from the maximum 6ft. I only ever did this once I'd reached sufficient flapping speed.

The results have been pretty tangible, I can tell you. From 6ft up and with my fastest flapping I can stay airborne anything from 0.37 to 0.46 seconds, depending upon wind speed. I imagine that once I get over that one-second barrier then the sky really will be the limit and there'll be no looking back.

I do hope you can write back with the details I have requested, as I would dearly like to spread my wings, as it were, before my 40th birthday (September).

I look forward to hearing from you soon.

Yours truly,

Terence Daly.

CHANNEL GLIDING CLUB 2002

Waldershare Park
Nr. Whitfield
Dover
Kent CT15 5NH
01304 824888

30th July 2004

Dear Mr Daly

If you wish to reach your 40th birthday, you should stop jumping off stepladders.

I enclose details of the more conventional means of getting airborne. You might consider contacting the Gliding Club at Ringmer, which is much closer to you. Their address is:

East Sussex Gliding Club
Kitson Field
The Broyle
Ringmer
East Sussex BN8 5AP
Tel 01825 840764

Yours sincerely

MC

Secretary

Alexander Literary, Film and Television Agency

148 Montpelier Road, Brighton, East Sussex, United Kingdom, BN1 2LQ.

The Prime Minister,
10 Downing Street,
London,
SW1A 2AA

Dear Sir,

I am writing to you on behalf of my Grandmother, Enid Galsworthy, who will be reaching the grand old age of 100 on the 15th of September this year. Enid has been a lifelong Labour supporter and is still very much compos mentis and up-to-date on political issues. When you finally came to power after eighteen years of Tory government it was, so Enid said, the happiest day of her life. She had closely followed your progress through the shadow government ranks and knew that you were the man for the job.

She is very excited that she will be receiving a letter from the Queen marking her centenary, but my family and I would like to make her birthday one that she will really remember. Would it be possible for you to write a brief letter thanking Enid for her lifelong support of the Labour Party? I know that she would treasure such a letter and she would undoubtedly think this the best birthday present she has ever received. You would be making a much-loved lady extremely happy in doing so. I think her cup would runneth over if you could also include a signed photograph as well.

When Enid was in her prime she was lucky enough to meet Humphrey Bogart at a charity event and found him to be a very charismatic and charming man. She was promised a signed photograph from Humphrey, but for whatever reasons she never received one. Might I suggest that if you can send a signed photograph to Enid you inscribe the photograph further with the phrase 'here's looking at you, kid'. This would, I think, kill two birds with one stone. She will be very, very surprised and extremely flattered.

If it is not possible for you to do either of the above then I'm sure that Enid will be entirely contented with her letter from the Queen - after all, she has no idea that I am writing this letter to you in the first place, so she will not be disappointed.

May I just take this opportunity also to congratulate you on what has been a renaissance in British politics, and to wish you all the best in the future for your government and equally importantly for your family.

Yours truly,

Guy Piran.

PS. If it is possible for the letter and/or the signed photograph could you please send these items through to my agency address, and I will ensure that they are suitably framed, etc, for her centenary celebrations.

1O DOWNING STREET
LONDON SW1A 2AA

From the Political Office

October 2004

Dear Mr Piran

I have been asked to thank you for your letter to the Prime Minister. I apologise for the delay in my response.

As requested I have pleasure in sending you a signed photograph of the Prime Minister for your Grandmother's 100th birthday.

With best wishes.

Yours sincerely

Rebecca Goff

REBECCA GOFF

Alexander Literary, Film and Television Agency

148 Montpelier Road, Brighton, East Sussex, United Kingdom, BN1 2LQ.

The Manager,
Islington Job Centre,
4 Upper Street,
Islington,
London,
N1 0MW

Dear Sir or Madam,

Am writing to you as the managing director of the agency representing the Spanish artist Manuel Sobrero. We have represented Manuel for a number of years and are sometimes called upon to help him organise installations and exhibitions. Manuel is very much what one would call a conceptual artist, and some of his artworks are extraordinarily abstract and surreal.

At the beginning of 2003 Manuel was commissioned to come up with an original and daring work of art for Covent Garden. Those commissioning the art wanted a piece that was ephemeral – that would be there for a day and then gone, never to reappear.

With this in mind we would like to use the employment centre to hire two people for one day. We will be paying £500 for the day's work. We require one male and one female between the ages of 35 and 45 who are not inhibited and are prepared to 'become' an art installation for the day.

Before they take up positions in the street they will be shaved to remove all body hair. They will then be smeared with copious amounts of bovine manure. They will then take up their positions in the main Covent Garden concourse. The male participant will then lay on top of the female for a period of six hours after which the roles will be reversed. Neither will need to have had any theatrical experience before but, as I'm sure you can readily understand, a strong extrovert character is essential.

I should be most grateful if you could get in touch with me as soon as possible to discuss this matter further.

Yours truly,

Guy Piran.

Islington Jobcentre Plus
4 Upper Street
London
N1 0NW

Friday 5th August 04

Guy Piran
148 Montpelier Road
Brighton
East Sussex
BN1 2LQ

Dear G. Piran.

Thank you for your letter, which I received on Tuesday 3rd August 2004, expressing your interest in placing a vacancy with Jobcentre Plus.

Since 2001 all handling of vacancies have been processed via our centralised vacancy teams, Employer Direct. Therefore in order to place your vacancy on our database, please be advised that you need to contact Employer direct on 0845 601 2001.

Please find enclosed an information pack, which will tell you all that you need to know about Jobcentre Plus services.

I hope the above information is enough to help fill your vacancy

Yours faithfully

Geeta Tailor
Vacancy Service Manager
Encl

BRIGHTHELM PRIMARY SCHOOL

148 Montpelier Road, Brighton, East Sussex, BN1 2LQ.

Fort William Tourist Information,
Cameron Centre,
Cameron Square,
Fort William,
TH33 6AJ

Dear Sir or Madam,

I am writing to you with the express purpose of getting some advice about Ben Nevis. In Easter next year another teacher and I will be travelling up to Scotland with a group of 25 5-6yr olds. They form the lower half of the Brighthelm Primary School here in Brighton.

Last Easter Day we held a sponsored egg and spoon race on Brighton Pier, which was a tremendous success and also raised some much-needed funds for the school. On Easter Day 2005 we would like to have yet another egg-and-spoon race up in Scotland. What we have in mind is to make use of Ben Nevis. What is the shortest route up and down the mountain? Is this shortest route the easiest in terms of climbing?

Most of our children are quite prepared for a strenuous challenge, but my colleague and I would still like to make it as easy as possible for the children to get up and down as quickly and easily as possible. I imagine that even with your quickest route it could still take a couple of hours or so. I'm also presuming that with it being Easter there will still be the possibility of a shower or two. What are the chances of this happening? For example, would you happen to have a record of what the weather has been like for the last few years on Easter Day? This will give my colleague and I some valuable statistics when it comes to considering whether to provide mackintoshes for our children or not (most mackintoshes are quite cumbersome and will get in the way of our children's egg-and-spoons!).

I don't think that there is anything else that we need to know, so I would be most grateful if you could just get back in touch with me with the information requested above.

Yours truly,

Mrs Anne Wayward. BA (Hons).

The Highlands
of Scotland
Tourist Board

Bord Turasachd Gaidhealtachd na h-Alba

Direct email: rod.johnston@host.co.uk 31 July 2004

Mrs A. Wayward,
Brighthelm Primary School,
148 Montpelier Road,
Brighton
BN1 2LQ

Dear Mrs Wayward,

<u>BEN NEVIS</u>

I refer to your undated letter, received here on 30th July, detailing your intention to run an event for 5 year olds on Ben Nevis at Easter next year. The contents of your letter give me grave concern and I find it difficult to believe that your letter is genuine.

As your correspondence does not give a telephone number I have tried to trace a contact number in order to speak to you personally, so serious are my concerns. There is however no trace or your school in any listings and my contacts in Brighton also have no knowledge of your establishment.

What you are proposing is extremely dangerous and irresponsible. Ben Nevis should not be tackled in winter by anyone other than experienced hill walkers and climbers. Snow can lie on the summit until June and Artic weather conditions can be expected on the Mountain anytime between October and May.

I cannot condone or support your event and suggest you find some other, less hazardous, method of raising funds. However if you should continue against this advice I feel it will be my responsibility to make public the contents of this letter.

Yours sincerely

R. D. Johnston
Tourist Information Centre Supervisor

148 Montpelier Rd,
Brighton,
East Sussex,
BN1 2LQ.

Speech Therapy Department,
Hammersmith Hospital,
Du Care Road,
London,
W12 0HS

Dear Sir or Madam,

I am writing to you as something of a last resort. I am 39 years old and work as an announcer at London Victoria train station. I have been in this position for some time now and I am very satisfied with the work that I do. Unfortunately it has been brought to my attention by my employers that I have unwittingly begun to repeat passenger messages at unwarranted times.

It has also been brought to my attention that I have begun to repeat the aforementioned messages before I have even finished enunciating the entire message in the first instance. This has led to a number of complaints from network passengers that I have begun to repeat the aforementioned messages before I have even finished enunciating the entire message in the first instance. This has led to a number of complaints from network passengers that I have begun to repeat the aforementioned messages before I have even finished enunciating the entire message by my employers that I have unwittingly begun to repeat passenger messages at unwarranted times.

I have just re-read the opening of my letter and I now realise that I am obviously doing exactly the same when it comes to the opening of my letter and I now realise that I am obviously the opening of my letter and I now realise that I am obviously doing exactly the same when it comes...Damn!

I should dearly like to know if I am suffering some sort of recognised disorder, and if I am suffering some sort of recognised disorder and further to this if, in fact, this disorder may in fact stem from the repetitive nature of my recognised disorder, and if I am suffering some sort of recognised disorder and further to this if, in fact, this disorder may in fact stem from the repetitive nature of my work.

I am pretty sure that the above will undoubtedly give you a reasonably detailed indication of the problems that I am having at the present time and that I have begun to repeat the aforementioned messages before I have even finished enunciating the entire message in the first instance.

Yours truly,

Benedict Tiscali.

Speech and Language Therapy Department

NHS Trust

Direct Line	:	020 8383 3076
Internal Line:		33076
Fax	:	020 8383 4667
E-Mail	:	hmclauchlan@hhnt.nhs.uk
Reference	:	HM/letters/TISCALI, Benedict
NHS No.	:	N/A

Hammersmith Hospital
Du Cane Road
London
W12 0HS

Tel: 020 8383 1000
Fax: 020 8383 3169

2nd August 2004

Benedict Tiscali
148 Montpelier Road
Brighton
East Sussex
BN1 2LQ

Dear Benedict Tiscali

Thank you for your enquiry regarding Speech and Language Therapy.

As you live outside our catchment area you are not eligible to be seen in this department. In this instance I would recommend contacting your local GP who will be able to refer you to the appropriate service in your area.

Yours sincerely

Helen McLauchlan
Speech and Language Therapist

Cc: SLT Filing Cabinet

BRIGHTHELM PRIMARY SCHOOL

148 Montpelier Road, Brighton, East Sussex, BN1 2LQ.

Carill Aviation Ltd.,
Building 2 (Cargo Hangar)
Southampton International Airport,
Southampton,
Hampshire
SO18 2NL.

Dear Sir or Madam,

I am writing to you as the headmistress of the Brighthelm Primary School here in Brighton. We are holding a number of sponsored events this year in order to raise much-needed funds for our school library. One of the events we are hoping to hold is a sponsored parachute jump involving twelve or so of our 4-6 year olds. The father of one of these children has come by a consignment of Russian Air Force fail-safe parachutes, and it was in discussion with this gentleman that we came up with the idea of the jump in the first place.

Apparently these parachutes open automatically with no need to pull any sort of opening chord. There is also a secondary back-up parachute that opens if the first parachute fails. What this means in essence is that we have a complete fail-safe system. Although some of our parents were dubious at first most are now completely reassured and are happy for their children to have a go.

What we have in mind is to hire a suitably sized aircraft and have it fly over the Isle of Wight. We would then jettison the children out at sufficient and safe time intervals. Because they are all young and inexperienced we would like them to be dropped at no higher height than 1000ft. This, incidentally, is the height that the parachutes open automatically, so the children will not have to go through any lengthy, and perhaps frightening freefall. When all our children are safely on the ground they will all use mobile phones to tell our ground-based teachers where they are. We will then reunited parents and children for an evening barbecue and disco.

Would you possibly be able to provide us with names and phone numbers of pilots who would be able to assist us in our worthy endeavour? We would hope that considering the sponsored nature of the jump there could be a little price reduction. I look forward to hearing from you in due course.

Yours truly,

Mrs Anne Wayward. BA (Hons).

CARILL AVIATION LTD

SOUTHAMPTON

AOC NO. 1146
FLYING TRAINING
SCENIC FLIGHTS
CHARTERS
AERIAL PHOTOGRAPHY

BUILDING 2 (CARGO HANGAR)
SOUTHAMPTON INTERNATIONAL AIRPORT
SOUTHAMPTON, HAMPSHIRE SO18 2NL
TEL/FAX: (023) 80 643528
TEL: (023) 80 627225

29 July 2004

Mrs Anne Wayward
Brighthelm Primary School
148 Montpelier Road
Brighton
East Sussex
BN1 2LQ

Dear Mrs Wayward

I have just received your extraordinary letter (undated) re parachute jumping for 4 year olds. !

It is obviously a wind up – but why? What are you actually looking for, apart from fund raising?

You have caught my attention with your joke – what next?

Yours sincerely

Caroline Rabson

EPC Rabson
Director / Chief Flying Instructor

148 Montpelier Road,
Brighton,
East Sussex,
BN1 2LQ.

Citizens Advice Bureau,
Lower Tanbridge Way,
Horsham,
West Sussex,
RH12 1PJ.

Dear Sir or Madam,

I am writing to you with the hope that you can offer me some sort of assistance and support. I am 67 and I have four children and eight grandchildren. I live in a pleasant flat here in Brighton and I lead quite an active social life. For example, I go to bingo once a week where I meet up with many of my best friends. We don't really go there to spend money but more to socialise (actually I did once win £100). I also like to go shopping with my daughter, Claire, as often as I am able. She's the most fun to go shopping with, as she still gets very excited when she finds a real bargain, and it really does put a smile on my face when she does. Sometimes she'll bring the grandchildren along too, in which case we always end the afternoon with ice creams at McDonalds.

I don't see my son very often as he works as an English teacher in Doncaster but he does keep in touch by letter and by phone, which is nice. I have to say I'm not terribly keen on Doncaster but I expect there are worse places to live and work (Hartlepool, perhaps, or even Hull!).

My Spaniel, Bruce, died a couple of years ago but I am still very fit so I got another young Spaniel who is called Roger. I thought that I'd never get over the death of Bruce but Roger has filled my life with joy and companionship once more. I also like to feed the pigeons in the park while Roger runs around chasing the squirrels. Those little fellows are extremely swift, as Roger is no slow coach when it comes to chasing. I hasten to add that he has never caught anything, other than a scratch on the nose from my neighbour's Siamese cat.

I haven't got a huge pension but it does pay for all the things I need and that is quite sufficient. My eldest daughter is a successful artist and has always been able to help me out when the occasion has risen. She even paid for my new Nissan Micra, which is a lovely little car with chequered seats with matching headrests.

I do hope you can get back in touch with me soon, as I am deeply concerned and worried.

Yours truly,

Edna Philips.

Horsham & District
Citizens Advice Bureau

Our Ref: BH/RM

If calling please ask for Beatrice Hobson   Tel. 01403 261916

02 August 2004

Mrs E Philips,
148 Montpelier Road,
Brighton,
East Sussex BN1 2LQ

Dear Mrs Philips,

Thank you for your letter which we received on the 28th July 2004, which gave us so much information about you and your family.

It would appear that your life, which you described to us so vividly, is full of interest and the activities which you tell us you undertake surely keep you fit and well.

We were sorry to hear about your dog Bruce, but you seem to have found a new companion in Roger and he seems to give you much pleasure.

You do, however, intimate that you are deeply concerned about a matter without telling us what exactly it is. We therefore cannot help you.

We would, however, suggest that you get in touch with the CAB in Brighton and Hove which is much nearer to you than we are. Their telephone number is 0845 120 3710 and the address
is: Brighton & Hove Citizens Advice Bureau,
       3rd Floor, Co-op Department Store,
       London Road,
       Brighton BN1 4LB

They may be able to help you sort out whatever it is that troubles you.

With very best wishes

Yours sincerely,

Mrs Beatrice Hobson,
District Manager.

Lower Tanbridge Way, Horsham, West Sussex RH12 1PJ

Advice Line: 0870 126 4080

Administration Line: 01403 261 916   Fax: 01403 218 548
www.horshamcab.org.uk Email: contact@horshamcab.org.uk
Registered Charity No 247389

Community
Legal Service

NATIONAL
LOTTERY
CHARITIES
BOARD

148 Montpelier Rd,
Brighton,
East Sussex,
BN1 2LQ.

Birmingham Royal Ballet,
Thorp Street,
Birmingham,
B5 4AU

Dear Sir or Madam,

I am writing to you as the mother of Charlene. Charlene has just turned eighteen and is a lovely girl. However, she has lately become quite withdrawn and depressed. There are probably a number of reasons why this has happened to Charlene, but the most likely reason is that she has become very conscious of her weight problem. Actually she has lost a little weight in recent months but she still weighs-in at just over 35 stone.

I think adolescent and teenage years are difficult years at the best of times, but when you have to contend with name-calling and bullying just because of your adipose tissue then it's even worse, isn't it?

My husband Gary and I have come up with a series of measures which we hope will bring Charlene out of herself a little and realise that there's a bigger world out there. That's why I'm writing to you now.

Would it be possible for Charlene to come and be a ballet dancer for the day? Charlene's grandmother is a very good seamstress and can make up a special tutu and costume for Charlene. Indeed, she has got pictures of a ballet dancer dressed up as a swan in a performance of Swan Lake and that's what we'd like Charlene to look like. We really think coming there for the day would do her the world of good. Having said that, we don't expect Charlene to suddenly want to be a ballet dancer or anything. I mean, to my knowledge she hasn't ever danced at all - even at school discos! We just want her to get to see a broader picture.

Both Gary and I would obviously accompany Charlene to monitor her day and to ensure that her nutritional requirements are met (she does have some specific dietary needs). We do hope that you can entertain our suggestion, and I can assure you that Charlene would be very well behaved and not be a problem to your staff or your dancers.

I hope you can write back soon and tell me of your decision.

Yours hopefully,

Brenda Blessed.

8th November 2004

**BIRMINGHAM
ROYAL BALLET**
Director David Bintley CBE

Brenda Blessed
148 Montpelier Road
BRIGHTON
BN1 2LQ

Dear Brenda

Thank you very much for your letter of 29th July. Please accept my apologies for this very late reply, but unfortunately your communication had dropped down the back of our radiator and we had to go to an awful lot of trouble with a wire coat hanger to retrieve it.

I am very sorry to hear of your daughter Charlene's predicament. We often get requests from what I will call the "bigger boned" young ladies who wish to become dancers, but there is a practical problem here, which though not insurmountable does put the onus back on the more muscular or densely packed adolescent.

The floors in our dance studios are specifically constructed to provide the dancers with the maximum amount of "spring." This is a complicated procedure that involves the delicate building of what is in essence a sprung floor; any undue amount of weight placed upon a floor like this means that the "springy" quality of the said floor is significantly reduced. At 35 stones, and your letter being written back in June does not take into account the summer break, which is the period when most of our young ladies put on a little bit more weight, Charlene is just that tiny bit "gravitationally challenged" for us to invite to spend a day with us. If she could be persuaded to drop, say 25 of those stones, then she might be in with a shout.

I am sorry to have to disappoint you, but I am sure you will understand that the structural well-being of our studios must remain of primary importance to me.

Best wishes

Yours sincerely

DAVID BINTLEY CBE

148 Montpelier Rd,
Brighton,
East Sussex,
UNITED KINGDOM
BN1 2LQ.

Brighton & Hove Citizens Advice Bureau,
Third Floor,
Co-op Department Store,
London Road,
Brighton,
BN1 4LB

Dear Sir or Madam

I am extremely concerned and agitated, and I am writing to seek your advice. Some months ago I went up to London to seek an 'alternative' remedy for my arthritic left leg. For many years now I have been troubled by rheumatism in the aforementioned leg, and all traditional medical treatments have been of little or no benefit.

It was my neighbour who first suggested 'alternative' treatment, and she put me in touch with a certain Charles Mbogo who is based in Tooting. Mr Mbogo hails from the Congo and purports to be a witchdoctor. I was hesitant at first to put my faith in Mr Mbogo, not least because I am a practising Christian. However, on my first visit to his home he assured me that there was nothing devilish about embarking on his curative course, and I duly visited him on eight subsequent occasions.

After these visits my leg did, indeed, seem to be in a much better state than it has been in years. I was able to bend my leg at the knee which I had not been able to do before. Not only this, but I was able to walk far greater distances than for many a long year. I have to say I was entirely happy and content with the outcome.

It was, however, on one of my newly liberated walks that something entirely untoward and uncanny occurred. Whilst strolling down Brighton promenade I bumped into an old friend of mine who just happened to have his 8 year-old granddaughter with him at the time. After five minutes of convivial chat, and with absolutely no conscious volition on my part, my left leg kicked the young girl up the behind sending her sprawling to the ground. Amidst floods of justifiable tears, my onetime friend angrily took his leave of me, even though I was apologising profusely for my involuntary actions.

Since then my left leg has kicked out at dogs, passing cyclists, potted plants, stationary and slow-moving vehicles, policemen, closed doors, and just last week my brand new television set.

I have tried in vain to contact Mr Mbogo but he seems to have mysteriously disappeared from his former residence.

I have given this situation a good deal of thought, and now the only conclusion that I can come to is that my left leg is in some way 'possessed'. I now deeply regret visiting an African witchdoctor and I am praying that you may be able to help me. Are you a priest qualified to perform exorcisms? If you are not could you put me in touch with one who can? I hasten to add that no other part of my body seems to be possessed whatsoever, and I have had no devilish thoughts or compulsions in terms of my mental state. It's just my damned left leg.

Is it possible to exorcise a leg on its own? If not, then I am more than happy to be fully exorcised from head to toe. I am even happy for my left leg to revert to the arthritic state it was in before I sought Mbogo's 'treatment' - at least then I'll be able to go out in public once again without insulting or injuring anyone further.

I do hope you can write back to me with your best advice as to my predicament.

Yours truly,

Charles Pickering. (Retired)

Brighton & Hove Citizens Advice Bureau

Third Floor, Co-op Department Store, London Road, Brighton BN1 4LB

Advice Line: 0845 120 3710
Fax: 01273 609038

Switchboard: 01273 696616
www.brightonhovecab.org.uk

Mr Charles Pickering (Retired)
148 Montpelier Road

Brighton

BN1 2LQ

Your ref:
Our ref:
Extension Number

30th November 2004

Brighton & Hove

City Council supported
Community
Legal Service

Dear Mr Pickering

Your letter seeking advice

Thank you for your letter dated 28th November concerning the unusual, yet unfortunate situation you have found yourself in.

As you may be aware the bureau prides itself on being able to offer advice on 'every' subject and, although we do not specifically have information in relation to leg related exorcisms, you may find some practical support by contacting the:

National Federation of Spiritual Healers
Old Manor Farm Studio
Church Street
Sunbury-on-Thames
Middlesex TW16 6RG

Tel: 01932 783164

In relation to the direct symptoms you have experienced, it would appear that your leg condition makes it difficult for you to walk. Although there are restrictions in relation to age (I note you are retired and if you are over 65 you need to claim Attendance Allowance), you may consider making a claim for Disability Living Allowance. You may be entitled to the lower rate of the mobility component if you are so severely physically disabled that you cannot walk outdoors on an unfamiliar route without guidance or supervision from another person most of the time.

We mainly have experience of helping clients whose conditions are related to every day occurrences such as back pain and work related injuries. Having said that, there is no specific regulation within Social Security law to prevent a claim on the basis of a 'bewitched' leg. It is our professional opinion that if you made a claim on such a basis, you should expect to be turned down, initially at least, and may have to make an appeal.

If the condition spreads from the leg to possess the rest of your body, your claim for Disability Living Allowance may become stronger.

I note that one of the consequences of your condition has been to damage your television set. You may be of the opinion that until your condition improves it is not worthwhile risking purchasing a further set. In this case it may be worthwhile seeking a refund for your licence. Although TV licensing does not often make refunds, they may find the unusual nature of your situation persuasive.

If you continue to kick vehicles, private property and especially policemen, you are likely to find yourself in trouble with the law. You may, therefore, wish to seek further help from a criminal solicitor. We do not have any knowledge of successful legal defences being launched which have been based on 'possessed legs', but from our experience solicitors tend to be an imaginative bunch and I am sure they will be able to help. You may now, therefore, wish to proceed to divert your attention in their direction with your problems.

Yours sincerely

Director

148 Montpelier Rd,
Brighton,
East Sussex,
BN1 2LQ.

UK Headquarters,
RSPB,
The Lodge,
Sandy,
Bedfordshire,
SG19 2DL

Dear Sir or Madam,

I am writing to you because I am very excited. I have been doing experiments for a long time, and now I have got some startling results.

You are not going to believe this but, after a large amount of crossbreeding, I have come up with a Dodo! I've only got one at the moment, but I hope to have a breeding pair in the near future.

I don't want to tell you exactly how I've done it (copyright, etc) but what I can tell you is that I've used capercaillie, chicken, turkey and emu in my unique 'birdy' mix. The emu bit was pretty hard, I can tell you, but the rest of the birds were relatively amenable.

Would you like to see my photographs? They show how I've ended up with a Dodo, including all the stages in between (breeding, crossbreeding, surgery, etc). When you see them you will realise what an important breakthrough this is.

I would like to see the Dodo reintroduced to the wild, *and* served up as a speciality dish – why not? If they breed well then there should be plenty to go round.

If you like, I could come to your HQ and give a lecture about what I've done. I have written to Channel 4 Television, and I think they will want to do a programme about me and my Dodos. That could be good publicity for everyone concerned.

Once I've done the Dodo I think I'd like to tackle some other extinct species. With my extensive experience and my experimental data I think I could bring back all sorts of things if I put my mind to it.

I very much look forward to hearing from you soon.

Yours truly,

David Arwin.

for birds
for people
for ever

UK Headquarters
The Lodge, Sandy
Bedfordshire SG19 2DL
Tel: 01767 680551
Fax: 01767 692365
DX 47804 SANDY
www.rspb.org.uk

Mr D Arwin
148 Montpelier Road
Brighton
East Sussex
BN1 2LQ

11 August 2004

Dear Mr Arwin

Thank you very much for your letter concerning the amazing results you have
achieved after crossbreeding a selection of birds.

This is a startling achievement and will, I am sure, create worldwide interest.
Although many colleagues are rather sceptical about the likelihood of a dodo being
re-created bearing in mind the recipe you have used – they can quite understand that
the emu bit was pretty hard – I would welcome the opportunity of viewing the
photographs. I am sure that the government on Mauritius will be delighted to hear
that their most famous inhabitant can live once more. Natural history museums
throughout the world will be falling over one another to view this amazing creature
as they only have incomplete skeletons. Although the dodo was eaten by the sailors
who discovered it, it looks a tough old bird to me. Perhaps it was desperation that
drove them to hunt it rather than its culinary delights. I am curious though, about its
diet, as I know that it thrived on the seeds of the calbaria major. These only
germinate once they have passed through the dodo's digestive system; the
destruction of these forest being a prime cause of its demise.

My only concern is that the dodo is a lesson in extinction and if extinct creatures
become easy to re-create then the need and desire to conserve them disappears with
dire consequences for us all.

Good luck with your continuing experiment and I am looking forward to seeing the
results on Channel 4 Television.

Yours sincerely

Valerie Osborne

Valerie Osborne
Wildlife Enquiries

BirdLife
INTERNATIONAL

Patron Her Majesty the Queen Chairman of Council Professor Ian Newton OBE FRS Chief Executive Graham Wynne CBE

Registered charity no 207076   640-0061-04-05

148 Montpelier Rd,
Brighton,
East Sussex,
BN1 2LQ.

Santa Claus,
Santa Claus House,
101 St Nicholas Drive,
North Pole
AK 99705

Dear Santa Claus,

I am writing to you as a last resort! I am 43 and live in Brighton, England, with my wife and three children. I stumbled into marriage without giving it the proper amount of thought and I now find myself working 9 to 5 to support a thoroughly unpleasant, not to mention hirsute, wife and three thoroughly obnoxious offspring. I have been through an inordinate amount of expensive therapy which has been of little or no use, and now all I long for is release from this dumb prison within which I find myself.

Would it be possible for you to take away my present family and replace it with one more in keeping with my temperament? I am not particularly attractive, so I'm not looking for any Marilyn Monroe replacement. As for the children, a straight swap for three girls to replace the three boys would be entirely adequate.

I know this request must seem almost absurd but I am at my wit's end.

Yours faithfully,

Guy Piran.

Dear friend

It was lovely to read your letter and I hope you have been good this year.

All the elves and helpers have been very busy making this card for you to play with. You'll need to help me remember to call at your house by colouring in the 'Santa stop here' sign and displaying it in your window. There are also some toys to carefully press out and play with.

I get very hungry on my travels around the houses so it would be a lovely treat for me if you could leave a small piece of food, maybe a mince pie, in the sleigh on your window sill next to your 'Santa stop here' sign.

A very Merry Christmas to you.

Love Santa. x

The Tragedy Store

148 Montpelier Rd, Brighton, East Sussex, United Kingdom, BN1 2LQ

25/11/04

The Comedy Store,
66 Rivington Street,
Shoreditch,
London,
EC2

Dear Sir or Madam,

My colleagues and I have just started a new type of club night, and we are hoping to use the Comedy Store as our venue. Just like the Comedy Store, the Tragedy Store will be bringing into town performers from all over the UK and from even further a-field.

Indeed, friends of ours in the United States have been running a successful Tragedy Club in New York for nearly a decade. Their popularity stems from club nights acting as a purgative experience for any audience. Many people who come to one of these events, feeling even in the slightest way unfortunate in life, often realise just how petty their misfortunes are in comparison to any of the performers. A number of more empathic members of the audience are often reduced to tears by this experience.

In terms of these aforementioned performers we would be hoping to have one of the 'heavyweights' of the American club scene flown over for the opening night of the Tragedy Store. Sally Bowls has been a manic-depressive all her life and on top of this has developed a number of social phobias, including an agoraphobic fear of audiences. Americans have been enthralled by her evident near-hysterical fear at being out there in front of them, virtually unable to stand, let alone speak. We would definitely want her topping the bill, and below her we have in mind as performers for our first night, Australian-born Gary Flowers who lost the bottom half of his body in a shark attack and has never come to terms with it; Local man Bill Setton who is a true misanthrope and rails against anything and everyone; and Emily Curzon who has never smiled or laughed in her life and will break into tears over the most minor of matters.

All in all we definitely think we will be offering London audiences a first night they will positively remember, and in general a new and exciting club night on the already burgeoning scene.

If you could get back to me at our agency address above I would be most grateful. I am positive that we can offer you full houses for our club nights and we would of course undertake all advertising for these events ourselves.

Yours truly,

Penelope Scanwell

Ms Penelope Scarwell
The Tragedy Store
148 Montpelier Road
BRIGHTON
East Sussex
BN1 2LQ

1st December 2004

Dear Ms Scarwell

Thank you for your letter dated 25th November regarding your *Tragedy Store* shows.

Before considering your proposal further, I should appreciate more details and a video tape would help. Also, I would need to meet you to discuss your proposal in further detail.

I can be contacted via my secretary, Yvonne on the numbers given below, or by email – don@thecomedystore.co.uk

Yours sincerely

Don Ward
Producer & Managing Director

148 Montpelier Rd,
Brighton,
East Sussex,
BN1 2LQ.

1/12/04

Adrienne Chinn Design Company Ltd,
Suite c216 Trident Business Centre,
89 Bickersteth Rd,
London,
SW17 9SH

Dear Madam,

I am writing to you to ask whether it would be possible for you to visit me and provide me with a quote for work which I would like done to my property. The house that I live in at present is a spacious two-bedroom terraced cottage with bathroom, kitchen and separate WC. There is also a small amount of cupboard space under the stairs.

What I have in mind is to have some clever partitioning done to maximise the utilised space of the cottage. Ideally I would like to have the upstairs bedroom space partitioned into ten separate bijou apartments all with en-suite showers. To maximise the space I would also like to have beds that fold up into the partitioned walls.

The downstairs living room, being of a good size, I would like partitioned into four separate offices. If possible I would also like to leave enough room to develop into a separate hospitality area with plumbing for a chikoozi and sauna.

With ten separate shower suites upstairs, I would then like to redevelop the existing bathroom and WC into an indoor cinema and/or bowling complex. With any luck there may be enough room after this partitioning for a small bar area.

At present I have no plans for the space under the stairs, but perhaps when you visit you may be able to suggest something yourselves.

I do hope you can get back to me on this as soon as possible, as, once the work is completed, I will be hoping to market the property.

Yours truly,

Mark Harrington.

ADRIENNE CHINN DESIGN COMPANY LTD.

INTERIOR DESIGN

www.adriennechinn.co.uk

Mr Mark Harrington   7th December 2004
148 Montpelier Road
Brighton
East Sussex, BN1 2LQ

RE: Your Letter Dated 1st December 2004

Dear Mr Harrington

Thank you for your letter outlining the proposed development of 148 Montpelier Road.

The most important factor concerning a renovation of this scope is compliance with Building Control Regulations. In particular we feel that Fire Regulations may be very strict concerning the number of occupants in the upstairs space.

We would therefore suggest that you arrange meetings with your local council's Planning Officer and local Fire Prevention Officer to discuss the feasibility of the works under consideration.

Only then would it be advisable to appoint your chosen designer.

Yours sincerely

Melvyn Fickling
Operations Manager

SUITE C216, TRIDENT BUSINESS CENTRE, 89 BICKERSTETH ROAD, LONDON SW17 9SH

T: 020 8516 7783   F: 020 8516 7785   E: info@adriennechinn.co.uk

COMPANY REGISTERED IN ENGLAND No: 2788573
REGISTERED ADDRESS: FIRST FLOOR, 60 RETHERDON ROAD, LONDON SW17 8QG
VAT REGISTRATION No: 735 7737 01

148 Montpelier Rd,
Brighton,
East Sussex,
BN1 2LQ.

25/11/04

Dr Penny Harvey,
Dept. of Social Anthropology,
Roscoe Building,
Brunswick Street,
Manchester,
M13 9PL

Dear Madam,

I am writing to you as the despairing parent of my seven-year-old son Timothy.
Timothy has recently been informed by his biology teacher at school that new
scientific discoveries have indicated that human beings have not, in fact, evolved from
the apes as previously thought, but actually from dinosaurs! Apparently this now
explains the disappearance of dinosaurs - they never did actually disappear at all
because they evolved into us.

I have to say that I have never heard such tosh in all my days. I wonder where on Earth
some of these so-called teachers come from. Are they plucked from the very dregs of
the intellectual bucket, so to speak?

What I find disgraceful is that notions as ridiculous as this are being transmitted to
young and impressionable children like Timothy. At this moment in time Timothy
won't hear a word said against his teacher's theory. Worse than this, every time I try to
discuss this matter sensibly with him he just jumps around the room gesturing like a
monkey and laughing at me. Last night I got into bed only to find a banana tucked
between the sheets.

I am not prepared to be made a monkey of by some third rate biology teacher from
Scunthorpe, and that is why I am writing to you. Would it be possible to bring some
much-needed sanity to this situation and write back to me indicating, in whatever
detail you feel is necessary, a 'real' and viable evolutionary theory. I should dearly
like to show this letter to Timothy in order to rid him of the belief that he is in fact
descended from a T-Rex.

I do hope you can take the time to respond to this letter.

Yours truly,

Miriam Cohen.

School of Social Sciences
The University of Manchester
Oxford Road
Manchester
M13 9PL

tel +44(0)161 306 1340
www.manchester.ac.uk

15th December, 2004

Dear Miriam,

Thank you so much for your truly wonderful letter – I have to confess that my sympathies with your frustrations were quite surpassed by my admiration for Timothy's sense of humour – his jaunts are truly worthy of Darwin's contemporaries who while they hadn't managed to think up the dinosaur theory, certainly turned their wits to banana jokes.

As to the substantive issue of our supposed descent from dinosaurs I agree that it is quite incredible – although unfortunately as you so graphically describe credibility is quite a different matter when you are a seven year old boy – and teachers always know best!

I have passed your letter on to a former colleague who is a world expert in evolutionary theory – thinking that he might have some of the early cartoons to pass on to Timothy – he is also a great communicator (with a 10 year old daughter) and I'm hoping that over Christmas he will amuse himself by composing a suitable reply to Timothy himself.

I think you should send your letter to the Times (or at least the Times Educational Supplement) – it would allow you to make your point, and bring a smile to many a frustrated parent.

I'm sure Timothy will prove to be more than a match for his teachers – I'd love to witness his derision when he moves beyond the dinosaur phase.

With best wishes,

Yours sincerely,

Penny Harvey

225

148 Montpelier Rd,
Brighton,
East Sussex,
BN1 2LQ.

The Spanish Embassy,
39 Chesham Place,
London.

Dear Sir or Madam,

I am writing to you as the chairman of the 'English Wars Re-Enactment Society', based here in Sussex. As part of a spectacular series of events planned for the summer of 2005 we are hoping to stage a re-enactment of the sinking of the Spanish Armada off the Sussex coast near Brighton. We are receiving lottery funding for this, and a number of wealthy patrons are also contributing to the significant cost of staging this event.

What we are hoping to do is to hire in real Spaniards to man the Spanish fleet. We feel that this will make for a much more authentic experience. Would you be able to provide us with details of employment agencies in Spain? We would be hoping to acquire about 750 Spaniards. There will be no need for them to have had sailing experience as they are only going to be there in token, prior to their respective boats being sunk. All such Spaniards will be issued with lifejackets before the battle commences. Once their boats have sunk they will simply be fished out of the water by one of our command vessels that will be on standby throughout the day.

There will, of course, be no real artillery used whatsoever. The entire English fleet's canons will all be loaded with blanks. These blanks sound like the real thing but are entirely harmless. The actual sinking of the Spanish Fleet will be controlled by remote control from one of the support vessels.

Our society is tremendously excited at this rare opportunity afforded us to re-enact one of the great battles of history .

All Spaniards hired for the event will receive a generous weekend allowance and have all their bus and ferry travel paid for. In addition to this they will be offered half - board lodging at a number of bed and breakfasts in Brighton. At the end of the day when everyone is safely accounted for, we are hoping to hold a large disco on the beach with a barbecue for ticket-holders. We sincerely believe that this is going to be a fun-filled event and one which the participants will remember for a very long time.

If you could reply as to the enquiry regarding Spanish employment agencies I would be most grateful. A colleague of mine has just suggested that I ask you whether or not you might actually have a 'Spanish Wars Re-Enactment Society'. Could this be the case? I suspect not. I don't think you modern Spanish are half as interested in wars (past and present) as we Brits are.

Thank you for taking the time to read this letter and I hope you can respond to our requests as soon as possible.

Yours truly,

Guy Piran.

SPANISH EMBASSY
LONDON

LABOUR AND SOCIAL AFFAIRS OFFICE

O. ref.: UDI/AS
Date: 10/12/04

Mr. Guy Piran
148 Montpelier Road
Brighton
East Sussex BN1 2LQ

Dear Mr. Piran,

I refer to your letter of 24th instant to the Spanish Embassy, requesting some information concerning the employment of Spaniards for the re-enactment of the sinking of the Armada, which has just been passed on to me for attention.

To that purpose, I am sending you a list of temporary employment agencies in the region where more re-enactment take place in Spain: Valencia, Castellón de la Plana and Alicante. In those areas they will know what you are talking about when you contact them. English language is also more common in those areas.

Yours sincerely,

Bernardo Fernández
Labour and Social Affaire Counsellor.

THE NARNIA'S FOR REAL COLLECTIVE

148 Montpelier Road, Brighton, East Sussex, United Kingdom, BN1 2LQ.

1/12/04

Amethyst Accomodation Ltd,
10 Sheppard Street,
Swindon,
SN1 5DB

Dear Sir or Madam,

I am writing to you as the chairman of the 'Narnia's For Real' collective based here in the United Kingdom. Boasting members from all over the world, we are hoping to organize a group-stay at your hotel during the second week of June 2005. Would you have an opening for about twenty-five of us during this week? We will not necessarily need twenty-five separate rooms. Indeed, if push comes to shove, we can actually make do with just one room, if that is all that you have available.

There is one request that we do have, however, without which our stay would be severely compromised. We would be hoping to bring our very own wardrobe with us, which is of a mahogany construct and measures approximately 7ft x 7ft x 3ft. This has proved to be something of an inconvenience to smaller hotels in the past, but we are hoping that as a larger hotel you may very well be able to accommodate us.

Once the aforementioned wardrobe is in place we can guarantee you that as a party we will be of little or no inconvenience to you. And even though all our party will be spending many years battling the forces of the White Witch and her demonic entourage, we still envisage that we'll all be back at just about the time that we set off in order to have a good night's sleep before a full continental breakfast in the morning.

We do hope that you will have accommodation available on the above dates, and please do not hesitate to contact me if you have any questions that you would like clarified.

Yours truly,

Edmund Caspian.

Amethyst Accommodation LTD

13/12/04

The Narnia's For Real Collection
148 Montpelier Road,
Brighton, East Sussex
BN1 2LQ

Dear Edmund

Thank you for your letter dated 01/12/04 regarding possible accommodation requirements during the second week of June 2005.

I have noted your comments with interest, but unfortunately we are fully booked at that time due to the Snow Queen and her entourage staying with us.

I apologise for any disappointment this may cause.

Yours sincerely

Carol Roberts
Communication Manager

148 Montpelier Rd,
Brighton,
East Sussex,
United Kingdom,
BN1 2LQ.

29/11/04

Birmingham Royal Ballet,
Thorp Street,
Birmingham,
B5 4AU

Dear Sir or Madam,

I am writing to you to offer you the opportunity of acquiring my new ballet production entitled 'True Blue'. It has taken me a great deal of time and effort to come up with this particular ballet, and I really believe that it could have the crowds flocking in to see it - and not just your 'typical' ballet aficionado's too!

True Blue is set in a mythical present where the whole country is under the tyranny of a mad dominatrix called Maggie Thatchless. Under this tyranny she forces everyone to undergo severe spanking and/or flagellation. Sometimes she even has her subjects put into bondage via the use of chains and ropes.

One of my favorite bits is where the good prince Tony Titters tries to get away from his bondaged imprisonment and ends up hopping about the stage with his one 'free' leg (the other leg will be strapped up behind his back along with both arms). I think it will be quite an awesome sight. I also think that having everyone perform absolutely naked apart from tiny 'mock' tutus will be quite a departure for any ballet company.

Not being a 'professional' ballet dancer myself I am a little concerned about the male genitalia in their liberated form. Is it possible for free-flying genitalia to come to harm? If so, then perhaps the males could wear supporting 'cock-socks' for moments of extreme agitation and/or bondage, flagellation, enemas, etc.

Suffice it to say that wicked Maggie Thatchless comes a cropper in the end and gets to taste the rough end of some of her own dirty medicine. I initially thought about crucifixion but then realized that this could offend any clergy present in the audience. That's why I've settled for boiling in oil, with all the attendant screams!

I know you are going to be interested in looking at the score for this ballet and, if you like, I can also send you some amateur footage that I've made to give you a good idea of how I really see this ballet being produced. I've had to do all the ballet moves myself, filmed with my video camera mounted on a tripod. Most of the time I'm in shot, but when I get a little carried away then I have a tendency to move out of shot temporarily. It's very hard to film yourself, especially whilst doing ballet. One thing I will say, however, is that I have actually had no trouble with my genitalia banging about, so to speak - but then they're not what you'd call enormous!

I very much look forward to hearing from you with a suggested timetable as to how you want to approach this. I'd be more than happy to meet up with you at the earliest opportunity. Thanks for your time and I look forward to hearing from you soon.

Yours truly,

Arthur Smitherington (Retired).

8th November 2004

BIRMINGHAM
ROYAL BALLET
Director David Bintley CBE

Arthur Smitherington
148 Montpelier Road
BRIGHTON
BN1 2LQ

Dear Mr Smitherington

Thank you very much for your recent letter and for the offer to mount your ballet, *True Blue*. Unfortunately I feel that most of the material in your scenario has been covered by me in my 1992 ballet, *Tory! Tory! Tory!*

Nudity in live performance is not something that we at Birmingham Royal Ballet approve of, although it does admittedly have the advantage of putting bums on seats. The problem is then getting the bums out of the seats, as they usually don't have a place to sleep at night.

Incidentally, the founder of the Royal Ballet herself, the great Dame Ninette de Valois never liked the spectacle of men dancing naked; she always claimed that they didn't stop moving when the music stopped.

Thank you very much for your interest.

Best wishes

Yours sincerely

DAVID BINTLEY CBE
Director

Direct dial: +44 (0) 121 245 3519
E-mail: DavidBintley@brb.org.uk
Department fax: +44 (0) 121 245 3570

148 Montpelier Rd,
Brighton,
East Sussex,
BN1 2LQ.

Brixtongue Poetry Night,
C/o Brixton Art Gallery,
35 Brixton Station Rd,
London,
SW9 8PB

Dear Sir or Madam,

I am writing to you as head of the Silent Poets Initiative based here in Brighton. We have been established now for over three years and boast a membership of over a hundred, including some members from as far a-field as Brisbane and Guadeloupe. In Brighton we run a weekly event where members and guests silently recite their poems to an audience. These evenings are now more popular than ever, and it is with this in mind that I am writing to you.

Would you be interested in hosting a competition night at your venue? What we have in mind is to have a panel of judges made-up from long-standing society members. They would be judging each competitors performance in terms of general demeanour and sensibility; how much empathic eye contact they each have with the audience; and emotional commitment to the reading itself.

Although self-composed verse is very much preferred it will also be possible for competitors to enter with recitations of, for example, Shakespeare or Spike Milligan. However, all competitors will be subject to the scrutiny of a number of invigilating lip-readers drawn from the Deaf Association. It may come as a surprise, but in the past we have had impostors who have entered our competitions with no 'real' poetry to recite, and who instead recite 'silent gibberish'. To many people's consternation one of these impostors, who was a second year student on a Performing Arts course at Brighton University, actually came second in a competition held in 2001. The Deaf Association representatives have insured since that day that there can be no possible chance of such cheating being repeated.

We imagine that a good number of members of our initiative would make the journey up to London for the competition, and we would warmly invite any of your regular poets to enter into the spirit of things and take part in the competition.

The winner, by the way, will receive a cheque for £100 and an engraved rose bowl. The second prize will be a cheque for £50 and the third prize a cheque for £25.

If you could get back in touch with me soon I would be most grateful, as we are hoping to organise this event in the coming few months.

Yours truly,

Pauline Abba.

BRIXTON ART GALLERY

35 BRIXTON STATION ROAD
LONDON SW 9 8PB
020 7733 6957
www.brixtonartgallery.co.uk

12th December 2004

Dear Pauline Abba,

Thank you very much for your letter dated 25th November regarding holding a competition night at the Brixton Art Gallery.

We would be very happy to host your event. Our usual rate for gallery hire is £40 an hour for seminars and workshops or £90 an hour for social events but for the Silent Poets Initiative we would be willing to let you use the gallery for free, if Brixton Art Gallery could charge on the door and provide food and drink.

A fuller account of the gallery space, photographs, and layout diagram are available on the Brixton Art Gallery website.

We will gladly publicise your event through the gallery website and through our mailout list to those who have attended our bimonthly performance poetry night 'Brixtongue'. Publicity materials like posters, flyers, press releases etc would however have to be provided by the Silent Poets Initiative. Brixton Art Gallery can send publicity to 25 local listings organisations in London but any further publicity would have to be organised by the Silent Poets Initiative.

We are holding our next 'Brixtongue' on Saturday February 12th so your own event should probably not be within two weeks of that event.

We look forward to hearing from you, with suggested dates and any particular needs or further information you might have. Your e mail address would also be of great use in speeding up communications.

Yours sincerely,

G. Parker.

G. Parker (Director, Brixton Art Gallery)

148 Montpelier Rd,
Brighton,
East Sussex,
BN1 2LQ.

Dearest MENSA,

Hello to you. I want you to help me if you could. I am not a very clever bunny when
I'm honest with no qualifications or nothing. I am bright with sparks and all that but
not with problems. My friend has told me you deal with Einsteins and this and that and
give people numbers for their brains. Some brains are big numbers aren't they. I bet I
am not huge and you can say that again. But my friend has told me you have another
place for little numbers. Is this true at all. He says it is called DUNSA and is a nice
club with easy positions and parties. Me and MENSA would not be happy but me and
DUNSA will be free and happy I think. I really want to join if I can. I am not
employed with money so will I pass the test. Will you help for me to get in. I am quite
jokey and fat if this will help me with the numbers. I love you to write back soon then
I can get out more.

Thanyou'

Guy Piran.

Mensa
The High IQ Society

British Mensa Limited
St. John's House
St. John's Square
Wolverhampton
WV2 4AH

Tel: 01902 772271
Fax: 01902 392500

enquiries@mensa.org.uk
www.mensa.org.uk

Registered No.
971663 England.

Guy Piran
148 Montpelier Road
Brighton
EAST SUSSEX
BN1 2LQ

29th July 2004

Reference: LE
Response No: 103795

Dear Guy Piran

Thank you for your recent enquiry about Mensa.

I am pleased to send you a brochure about the society, as well as a Home Test for you to complete and return for marking. This is your first step towards membership of the high IQ society.

Before starting the test, please take the time to read the instructions carefully. These can be found on the inside front cover. When you have done the test, please complete the payment form (back cover), adding your unique response number (top right of this letter) and return it in the pre-paid envelope provided.

We will mark your test in the strictest of confidence and send you the result within 21 days. This test will indicate whether your IQ is likely to fall within the top two per cent of the population – the criteria for gaining membership of Mensa. In that case you will be offered the chance to progress onto a full, supervised IQ test.

If you have any further questions about Mensa or the Home Test, please contact us on Freephone 0800 05 63672, anytime between 8.30am and 4.15pm. I do hope you will take the opportunity to complete the Home Test. It would give Mensa great pleasure to be able to welcome you into our society.

Yours sincerely

E. Southan

Eileen Southan - Membership Secretary

ENC